T0035506

Mary Giuliani is an inveterate people pleaser, a wonderful caterer, and an even better raconteur and storyteller. This memoir of bumbling happily upward through the travails of big city parenting, family life, and career might be her meatiest, most delightful creation yet. —Adam Platt, *New York Magazine*

Mary Giuliani is a brilliant storyteller. Following as she finds herself in crazy situations, I found myself laughing and inspired by her pluck, humility, and resilience. —Dana Cowin, founder, Speaking Broadly and former Editor in Chief of *Food & Wine*

How to Lose Friends and Influence No One is another fabulous collection of short stories from the brilliance that is Mary Giuliani. Her storytelling has the perfect alchemy of humor, soul, and depth. This creative is pure magic. You will not be able to put it down! I am absolutely ready for all of Mary's stories to be turned into films. Oh, and I love her. —Mindy Cohn, actor

A funny, and witty memoir that celebrates pop culture, parties, and pigs in a blanket. Mary muses about iconic TV stars of yesteryear who influenced (or who inadvertently raised) her, like Pinky Tuscadero, The Fonz, Jo from Facts of Life, Jack, Chrissy, Janet, Laverne, and Shirley. She has catered for and rubbed elbows with celebrities and racked up hilariously delicious anecdotes while on the job. Behind all the showbiz and passed hors d'oeuvres is a charming and graceful story about how Mary makes sense of life, survives, and keeps the party going no matter what. That's Showbiz.
—Murray Hill, Comedian, entertainer, actor

How to Lose Friends and Influence No One

Mary Giuliani

How to Lose Friends and Influence No One

Mary Giuliani

golden
NOTE
BOOK
PRESS
WOODSTOCK, NY

How to Lose Friends and Influence No One

First published in 2023 by Golden Notebook Press
Copyright © by Mary Giuliani

First Golden Notebook Press Printing: May 2023

Golden Notebook Press, LLC
29 Tinker Street
Woodstock, NY 12498

This book is a memoir. It reflects the author's present recollections of experiences over time. Some names and characteristics have been changed to protect the privacy of individuals, some events have been compressed, and some dialogue has been recreated.

goldennotebook.com
goldennotebookpress.com
@goldennotebookbookstore

ISBN: 978-0-9675541-3-6

Designed by James Conrad

Printed in the United States of America
1 3 5 7 9 10 8 6 4 2

First Edition

For Mom, Dad, and Nanette,
for signing off on the blueprints
of my dreams with your
unconditional love and support.

For Ryan and Gala, for making
all my very best dreams come true.

And

For you, yes you, please remember that
dreams have no expiration date.

Contents

The Zen of the Weinermobile

SUBJECT: NYC Caterer to the Stars and Author of *Tiny Hot Dogs* Seeks Position Driving the Oscar Mayer Wienermobile

I once applied to live in a hot dog. Tempted by an advertisement that came across my desk at precisely the right time, I guess you can say I was beginning to question just about everything in my life.

The years leading up to this extreme and slightly hilarious decision were spent building what I thought was #mybestlife. I went on not one but four glamorous vacations, partied with rock stars of stage and kitchen, had the most success in business that I'd ever achieved and seemingly got everything I had always wanted—and guess what? I was deeply unhappy.

As I filled out the very detailed application (FYI: you need a BA to drive a hot dog), I was convinced that this would be the answer for which I was searching. I was in a slump. Obviously, the hot dog driver position could be the answer to all of it. I could shrug all the responsibilities that came with being me, kidnap my daughter for a year (who was now almost four and joyfully and heartbreakingly growing up too fast), as well as my husband, who had been on the road constantly, working on his passion project. Just the three of us, living one life, in one place—a family reset if you will—albeit a place that was in fact a large vehicle shaped like a hot dog. I grew giddy, imagining the simplicity of this new imagined life.

But before I pressed SEND and committed my family to life in a mobile wiener, I decided that maybe a little introspection was in order, so I asked a pal of mine who had actually "seen the light" as part of her self-help journey, and, per her suggestion, packed my bags and headed to the gorgeous mountain range of the Berkshires in Western Massachusetts, home to the famed yoga and wellness center Kripalu.

On the drive up, I made a list of what had transpired which was leading me to this decision and it was no small list.

- three miscarriages
- became a mother via a surrogate
- published two books
- opened a food hall in the middle of Penn Station
- got sued
- assisted my husband in opening a restaurant and a hotel
- maintained my 400+ parties-a-year plus catering business
- lost my best friend to cancer
- lost my mentor to a public scandal
- gained 15 pounds
- and grew gray hair in places I didn't even know gray hair could grow

I checked into Kripalu for a yoga/juice cleanse. Yes, I know, the girl who has written two books about cocktails and hot dogs, who once ran around a party wearing nothing but a sensible sports blazer before diving head-first into a trashcan, who thinks that mozzarella sticks are the greatest contribution to American cuisine, yes, this person was going to fast on green juice and do yoga three times a day. For a whole week.

I was telling myself that going to the other extreme would make it all better. Makes sense, right?

Well, I lasted a total of twelve hours in the juice fast program until I made a break during a morning exhale and headed straight for the front desk to plead for my money back. Instead, the mindful receptionist talked me into joining another program that she promised would allow me to chew real food and since she made it very clear, in a namaste, no nonsense way that my money was non-refundable, I played along and reluctantly walked down the hallway and into a program, already in progress.

"We have a juice cleanse defector," was how I was greeted by the instructor, a delightful force of nature named Aruni, who had the lovability of Gilda Radner blended with the intelligence, wit, and wisdom of a wise guru who had seen things. And by that, I mean, real things.

I knew within moments of taking my spot on the floor that I was exactly where the universe wanted me to be. A place with nothing to do except this inner work, and no place to go, so my only options were to listen and receive. Wow, what a new concept for this small Italian who was constantly talking and incessantly giving in to others' needs without a thought of my own. In essence, I agreed that spending five long days in a room full of total strangers, from all walks of life, gathering in a share share circle, crying, and laughing, would be just what I needed.

It was during that week that Aruni asked one poignant question that rang so deeply in my ears, my teeth rattled. Essentially it was the simplest of queries: "What do *you* love?" Why was this a revelation to me? Because in that moment, I realized that most of my life, people kept telling me what I *should* love. You see, I was a child of both the Catholic Church and Dale Carnegie, meaning that by the age of ten, I was both God-fearing in the eyes of the Lord and highly effective in the eyes of Dale Carnegie. *How to Win Friends and Influence People* played incessantly on cassette tapes in my parents' car. From a young age, I understood that I was expected to make everyone love me, or at least, like and respect me. As I grew up, that desire deepened, and it might have been in that moment with Aruni when I broke with what others wanted for me and instead, loudly released into the universe what I wanted for me, which was this: to stop people pleasing, to stop saying "yes" when I meant "NO!" and, as I also realized with a start, to not fall into my usual habit of thinking that living healthy meant tossing aside all of what I enjoyed in favor of what I thought would be good for me. I mean, from hot dogs to juice cleanses? Was I crazy? I needed balance and I needed peace.

A week later, I left Kripalu with the motivation I needed to help me navigate my new vision. It seemed attainable. Hell, it seemed easy. Aruni had empowered me with the tools to stop, to be present, to be mindful. I could enjoy today for what it is, not for the promise of what may or may not ever come. And it worked, for a little while, until I felt myself reverting to old thinking, so, I went to the Oscar Mayer website, pulled up the saved application on my laptop and pressed SEND. At the end of the day, I felt it would just be easier to live in a hot dog.

I waited into the fall to hear back. Crickets. And while the hot dog never pulled up to my driveway and honked for us to come out and load up our bags, Covid arrived and with it, months of seclusion with nothing but my family and my thoughts. No work, no frantic scheduling, no need to even shower or get dressed. Kripalu EVERY DAY! A universal pause not just for my family, but for all.

Some people took (let's be honest here)

delusional advantage of this, saying, "Wow, here's that perfect opportunity to learn French, to learn to cook, to learn something new." I took it as a time to deeply examine, how the hell did I get here and why did I always want to run away from it all? Yes, I loved my life and my career, but it just needed to be . . . tweaked. Something big needed to happen—something bigger than repeat trips to wellness retreats or a cross country family kidnapping, master minded by me and sponsored by Oscar Mayer. I needed to reenter this world with appreciation, a stronger command of my voice, and the simplest way for me to do that was to continue to ask myself (as Aruni asked on that pivotal day), "What is it that *you* love?"

First, I was okay if not everyone loved me. With a combo of joyful liberation and maybe even a little shrug of my shoulders as in "who cares?" Second, I also realized that winning friends and influencing others was no longer part of my big plan. But would this stick? And what would come next? I had no idea, but I felt ready and hopeful. Which was a good thing, because as quarantine came to an end, I unfortunately had no other choice but to face this new day. Oscar Mayer got back to me . . . . Keep your day job, lady.

Swimming
With the Nuns

I should have known the moment I smelled the heady combo of quiche and Lysol. My mother frantically rushed around to clean our already perfectly spotless California (by way of Long Island, NY) ranch-style home. All the signs were there: The nuns were coming!

"Why are they coming here?" I asked. My mother was now basically Windexing our toy poodle Mona.

"Because it's nice for them to leave the convent every once in a while."

"Sure, I get that, but why always to our house? Why not Coney Island or The Catskill Game Farm or I don't know—anywhere else but our house?"

"Be nice, Mary, and go wash your face." Please note: I must have had a very dirty face growing up, because that is the one thing I remember my mom repeatedly asking me to do.

Up until this point, I had been doing a great job of keeping my troubles at school far off my parents' radar, but now with this invite, my mother was about to find out that her little angel had a very dusty halo.

As soon as those nuns waddled off that bus, the jig was up.

What was I so worried about? Well, put it this way, the nuns and I didn't exactly have the holiest of relationships.

My sister Nanette and I attended Catholic School and while I've said this before, it cannot be overstated: she was the good one and I was the "not so good" one. Catholic school was the place where these differences became exceedingly obvious.

While Nanette was working in class to maintain her perfect GPA (she graduated Valedictorian of the eighth grade), I spent most of my time not paying attention in class and instead doodled pictures of "the nuns" in my notebook and concocted ridiculous stories about them. I even gave them nicknames and was in general, utterly disrespectful in the eyes of The Lord. This was all before an ADHD diagnosis existed.

If Jesus had access to my notebook, He would no doubt compliment His Father for creating such a devilishly witty one. Or perhaps upon further inspection, He would quickly ascertain that the nuns had scared the sacred out of my precious little heart.

In the end, even with His ever-loving heart, Jesus would indeed learn that I was guilty of the worst schoolyard sin: the renaming of the sisters.

Sister Albert was Fat Albert. Every time I entered the Learning Center, I'd yell out, "Hey, hey, hey." Luckily for me, Sister Albert didn't watch TV.

Sister Christine was Weebles Wobble. She was at most five feet tall on a good day. She was round and small and actually did wobble, so I wasn't far off the mark. I got in trouble for doing her walk, when I dared to jump out of the single file line we were strictly ordered to follow. And when she turned around and caught me, I sang the Weebles TV commercial about the popular toy and encouraged my classmates to join in: "Weebles wobble but she never falls down."

Sister Joyce was Joyce Dewitt. First, because she resembled the actress and second, because *Three's Company* was my favorite show and her character Janet was my least favorite of the bunch. In fairness to Janet, I had a huge crush on Jack, so I wasn't that fond of Chrissy, the third of the roommates, either. Sister Joyce was very tall, had short hair, loved basketball and was a real ballbuster. She had the habit of faking heart attacks at the blackboard so that we'd rush up to her, concerned she was dying before our eyes.

Finally, there was our Principal, Sister Loraine, a.k.a. "Paper Tits." This was because she looked like she had crumbled two pieces of paper and stuffed them in her bra. I had the pleasure of sharing this nickname with her via Fat Albert who had confiscated my notebook.

My sister Nanette was Sister Loraine's "assistant," which meant that three times a week, she sat at a small desk perched outside Sister Loraine's office to check in the kids being sent in to see good ol' Paper Tits. Strange as it seems, Nanette never once returned my "high five" attempts that I tossed out while walking past her desk, before going in to get reprimanded by The Boss.

Now they were all coming to my house, to spend the afternoon with me and my mother. Since Nanette was working on her professional dance career, she was busy with afternoon classes that kept her late, so it was just me, mom and the nuns.

The doorbell drove me to sheer panic. Was my face clean?

My mother greeted them with total "Nance-ness." Nance-ness meant true love, warmth, and the sharing of everything in our blessed home to such a degree that guests left with whatever wasn't nailed down to the floor. My mother is a notoriously generous and amazing gift giver. Nance once gave a guest she had known for all of twenty-four hours one of her mink coats.

"Hello Mary."

"Hello Sister Christine," I replied in a Seinfeldian "Hello Newman" sneer.

These ladies were on my turf now. It was my mom who made them quiche. I felt like I was holding all the cards and maintained this tough posture throughout most of lunch by not meeting their gaze and responded to questions with one word answers. I sized them up with smirks and snarls as they ate our food and drank our wine.

"Mary, show the Sisters down to the pool."

Why me?

Unenthusiastically, I led the procession of nuns down the stairs, one by one in a single file but this time, they were behind me.

"You can change over there, the towels are outside, please don't run on the bluestone and you should really wait at least thirty minutes before using the diving board." With the rules established, I started to walk back upstairs

"Aren't you going to join us?" Sister Christine asked.

Surprised, I replied, "Well, okay. Let me show you where we keep the pool floats."

While they changed in the pool shed, I took my favorite spot on the tip of the diving board, which I decided would be my "power position." I wasn't sure of their angle here, but I was still game to be The Boss.

And then the visual I would never ever forget. First Fat Albert, then Joyce Dewitt and then Paper Tits . . . one by one . . . but not in a single file. For the first time, they were without their habits or the eighty-seven layers of clothing they usually donned, and I saw them as people, even though they all wore the same navy blue (what I assumed were God issued bathing suits with skirts). Sister Christine even wore a cute little white bathing cap with flowers on it.

But it wasn't just the outfits that threw me. It was their smiles, laughter and camaraderie. Dare I say, they even displayed a childlike playfulness. They appeared prettier, Fat Albert wasn't so fat, St. Joyce not as butch, Paper Tits, well, ok, she still had paper tits, but you hardly noticed them when she was smiling at you.

"Are you going to dive?" Sister Christine yelled from across the pool.

I stood up and took my best attempt at a swan dive. When I resurfaced they were all clapping and cheering. Sister Christine announced to the other nuns that I was so beautiful that they should call me Yellow Bird, inspired by my perfect bird-like dive and my yellow bathing suit. I was enchanted!

For the rest of the day, I proudly lived up to my new nickname Yellow Bird, and rejoiced every time they asked me to dive again and again. The nuns were having a blast and not one of them mentioned to my mother that I was a rotten little kid, or how much better my older sister was.

After an hour or so of this, the nuns helped my mom with her garden—though Nance was a great cook, she had no green thumb—and we completed the perfect day on the patio eating ice cream. I even talked Sister Albert into a quick game of catch. When it was time to go, my mother said her famous, "Wait!" She went down to the basement and grabbed a case of wine for them to take back to the convent.

Looking back, I wondered if Nance set up their visit to show me that the nuns were just regular people who could laugh and smile just like us. Maybe putting out a little generosity could show me, without telling me, what a little monster I could be.

By the way, it turned out not to be such a happy day for my dad, who, upon his return from the office, realized my mother had gifted the nuns with an extremely rare case of vintage pinot noir.

Now, lest you think my world had truly changed and I was suddenly transformed into the superstar student at school, think again. Back in school on Monday, I was gravely disappointed when Sister Christine called me Mary and not Yellow Bird; that Fat Albert didn't smile the same way she smiled in the pool and that the day of leisure did not cure Sister Joyce's fake heart attacks at the blackboard.

But I was still happy to share a secret with the sisters. It may have been the first time I understood the true pleasure of dropping your guard and letting in people considered strangers, people with whom you assumed you'd have nothing in common, only to realize there is so much that connects us if we just make room for it.

Also, I learned to always check the wine label before gifting.

The Food Network Hates You

"Hates me? Why?"

One night after a few martinis over dinner at "The Clubhouse"—our favorite restaurant in Greenwich Village—my good friend very bluntly delivered this news.

"They really didn't give me a clear answer. I just mentioned your name and that you would be great fit for a show they were discussing and the whole room in unison shouted, 'NO!' There may have even been a few emphatic hands thrown in the air."

When I pressed him for more information, I couldn't tell if that was really all the intel that my friend had, or if he was sparing my feelings by protecting me from similar very blunt feedback I had received from a talent agent during my early acting days, "You have talent but you don't have a face for television."

"Who hates you?" asked our waiter, a man we had all grown to love over the years, who I'm sure would defend my honor with all his Sicilian might, if given the chance in a room full of television executives.

How could they hate me? How could anyone hate me?

I was on *The Barefoot Contessa* years before she invited just about everyone to be a guest, including the oh-so-lovable Jennifer Garner, back when real legit, local business owners (known to no one outside the East Hampton community where Ina lives) were asked to join her in front of the camera. Doesn't that give me some real OG Food Network credit, if Ina personally anoints you before anyone else?

But as much as I pondered "why do they hate me," I couldn't really be that surprised as they had given me a few chances during the dozen or so meetings I had with them over the years, where I felt like I was killing it and then sat disappointed that nothing ever came from it. However, hate is a lot to digest, especially when it's coming from a place where the two things I love most not just collide, but in fact, reside: food and television.

By the time my friend finished his chicken parmesan, I was deflated. After many hard days of running my catering company, I would walk though Chelsea Market thinking, "one day . . . one day, that phone message, or email or puff of Vatican smoke from the Food Network will appear," inviting me upstairs (where their studios are located) to join their elusive club. The Food Network inviting you to join them in their studio feast that never ends is every food worker's dream. Who wouldn't fire up all burners for the chance to be beamed into millions of homes doing that very thing that you love?

But frankly, I don't think it was the Food Network that extinguished my burning souffle of desire. The Food Network didn't know what to do with me, because I didn't know what to do with me, thus activating my ever-present imposter syndrome. Since I did not attend culinary school or spend hours working in the kitchen prior to starting one of the most successful catering companies in New York City, I assume they, like others, had a hard time making the connection between Mary the Celebrity Caterer and Mary Who Doesn't Eat Fish.

And the doing what you love on TV part? Maybe they were onto me, because to be perfectly honest, I don't really love cooking as much as people think someone who owns a catering company should? Maybe they caught me saying to aspiring cookbook authors after my first book, "Want to lose your love for cooking? Write a cookbook."

Maybe I was pigeon-holed in that first idea I pitched them years ago: My Woodstock "party barn" concept with apron, high heels and copious recipes for cocktails, cocktails, and more cocktails. Come to think of it, I don't think there was any mention of food in my pitch. Then *At Home With Amy Sedaris* debuted and I threw up my hands and said, "Well, I guess that dream is over."

But instead of harping on he negative, I chose to focus on the positive, which included this train of thought: "Hey maybe I've been spared in some way, in that I'll never be confined to a signature puffy Mr. Softee hairdo or sports visor or annoying catch phrases.

Maybe the Food Network saw that my show ideas are a little less mainstream than the parent company preferred. Maybe they thought I beat my own drum a little too loudly. Maybe my love for the humble mozzarella stick was too much for them or maybe it did just come down to the simple truth—I'm not naturally skilled at cooking on television, because I did shoot twenty cooking videos for them pre-pandemic and the crowds did not go wild.

But just in case my friend was exaggerating your utter distain for me, hey Food Network or any network . . . how about some of these ideas:

The Pantless Contessa

Join this unpredictable hostess while she cooks, drinks, laughs, cries and sings all without wearing anything down south. You will leave this show with no real usable cooking skills, but you will learn things like what to do if one of your guests accidentally leaves with someone other than their spouse. *The Pantless Contessa* drinks as much as she cooks, which makes anything possible for this lovable curmudgeon, whose catchphrases include "Oh, then why don't you just cook it yourself?" and "Fuck if I know."

Recipes Before You Die

Do you have a loved one that is a great cook but doesn't write down any of their recipes? Are they over the age of eighty-five and staring down death's door? Well, then tune in to see old people on their last leg share the secrets for their famous veal picatta with their grandchildren who are only half listening while checking likes on Instagram.

Oy Goy

My Jewish-Italian cooking show idea. All the guilt, schmaltz and mozzarella you can pack into thirty minutes, with special guests like my personal heartthrobs, Mandy Patinkin and Alan Alda.

P.S. To be clear, my ideas are not limited to just television. How about my serious money making ideas, like "Car Toilet," which would be fully automatic or available with a less expensive manual option. Or, taking cues from *Baby Boom* I still think that "Baby Coat Check" is a brilliant, missed opportunity. How many times has your sitter canceled on you just before a big work meeting? "Baby Coat Check" allows you to focus on impressing the boss while someone else builds sugar packet monuments with your child behind the scenes.

You'll Be
Leaving Soon

One of the biggest struggles for me in life is setting up healthy social boundaries. For years, my husband described me as "Crazy Glue," which meant that mildly (sometimes deeply) insane people loved to attach themselves to me. The kind of people who would suck the life out of me until I was left depleted mentally, physically, financially, and, if they were really good, all of the above. My best friend calls it "Mary kibble," explaining: "It's like you have a special kibble in your pocket that attracts all types of stray kitties. Once they get a taste, they never want to leave." Things came to a head in 2005 when I moved to the Hudson Valley to take a break from my hectic city life. We fell in love with a small parcel of land with a tucked-away home, a rural property outside of town that once belonged to a writer for *The New Yorker*, where we planned to relax, recharge and unwind. However, in a matter of what felt like hours, my home became a gathering place for all the town "schnorrers." (Translation: Schnorrer is Yiddish word and means a freeloader who frequently asks for little things, like cigarettes or small sums of money, without offering anything in return.)

It was as if I hung a sign from my front door that read, "If you suffer from some type of narcissistic personality disorder, haven't worked in years, need money for your 'big idea,' are a smoker but don't buy your own cigarettes, then, come right in! You are more than welcome to sit in my yard and complain to me for hours about your brutal work life while I cook you dinner after coming off an eighty-plus hour city workweek. Or play on repeat how if only you had this amount of money, or that new laptop or access to five thousand dollars of investor seed money, then all your dreams would come true." Apparently, I was there to make all those dreams come true for them! Okay, I have to confess that I did have a sign on our front door that read

"Hippies Always Welcome" so maybe I was asking for it.

My husband would come home and throw up his hands in frustration when he found me holding court with a guest whose opening line was, "Can I take a shower?" and then ask for a towel as they headed off into our one bathroom. Another time, we found a woman buck naked and floating on one of our pool rafts, completely comfortable crashing our pool, because, as she explained to us, she had swum in our pool years before as a teenager.

"What are you doing?" Ryan once yelled as he saw me hauling a wheelbarrow of vegetables though our yard to help a "friend's" elaborate photo shoot, which I had permitted to take place, but "outside only."

"You do know she's in our kitchen, with her photographers shooting away, right?"

Yup, what a sucker I was.

I think the *piece de resistance* was the time I agreed to let a local painter take over our barn. We had met this painter at a town bar and after a few drinks, we were fast chums. I became completely captivated by the idea that our barn, which had once been a studio for a respected well-known artist, could once again be the center of the Woodstock arts community. I envisioned welcoming a rotating roster of local creatives to use our barn as both studio and gallery space. So my new pal was to be the first "artist in residence." He'd create a body of work in our barn and debut it to the community and the world, and my catering company would throw the most incredible opening parties for him, and others to come, the most exciting soirees ever seen in the Hudson Valley. A few days later I instantly knew something was off when we pulled up to our house just in time to see the artist coming back around from the side of the barn, pulling up his pants. As the barn didn't have plumbing, he had taken a plastic bag out bag out back and—well, you get the idea.

"Mary!" hissed my husband. "Is this guy living in the barn?!"

"Don't be ridiculous," I said.

But Ryan was correct. The artist had in fact rented out his own home and was basically squatting in, as well as behind, our barn. A week later, Ryan told him to pack up his canvases, his blankets and his plastic bags.

I think Ryan was particularly astounded by my lack of boundaries as a first-time homeowner. As I am my father's daughter and Dad is notorious for kicking people out of his home (even including my husband), once he feels they have overstayed their welcome, out they go.

Here's a classic Dad move. Let's say you've been in residence for the weekend and by Sunday morning, he's deemed that he's had enough of you. He'll come over to you while you're eating breakfast. He'll look at you. He'll make this inquisitive little face, which shows you he is very interested in what he's about to discuss with you, but be warned, he's a sneaky one.

"You had a good time? You enjoyed yourself here? That's good. When you're finished eating, you'll be going upstairs, and you're going to get your bag and then you'll be leaving soon."

We even have a family phrase for it: "Don't be a Mrs. Doyle."

My grandfather Franklin was a handsome man and when he died, several women showed up to the funeral home, claiming to be his girlfriend, as did a bunch of men wearing very silly hats with feathers on top. It turns out my grandfather was both a ladies' man and a member of the Knights of Columbus. The only woman we personally knew was Mrs. Doyle, who was eighty at the time, and therefore she was the only one my parents invited back to our home after the funeral. A huge snowstorm was just starting so my parents felt she'd be safest spending the night before driving back to who-knows-where.

Did Mrs. Doyle think that this was an invitation to live at our house forever? Well, she might have. In fact, why wouldn't she? My mom turned down her bed that night. She gave her a nice little housecoat to wear. And the next morning, she laid out a huge breakfast with freshly squeezed orange juice and a pot of hot coffee. Mrs. Doyle was in heaven. I was sitting next to Mrs. Doyle at breakfast and was reminded of the scene in the musical *Annie* when Annie goes to Daddy Warbucks' mansion for the first time and starts singing, "I Think I'm Gonna Like It Here." I could see Mrs. Doyle sort of looking around and sizing up the situation. I could almost hear her thinking (also to the tune of "I Think I'm Gonna Like It Here") "No need to change my own Depends. They will puree my food for me."

My father must've noticed this too because when I looked up, I saw that look on his face. I knew what was about to go down. He had had enough of Mrs. Doyle and it was time for her to go. My father got up from the breakfast table and walked over to her.

"Mrs. Doyle, you had a nice stay here? Good, good. Well, we're going to get you in your car and get you on the road."

"But Robert," Mrs. Doyle stammered,

"do you think the roads are clear yet?"

This was lost on deaf ears, because before Mrs. Doyle could finish her query, my dad went upstairs and soon returned with her suitcase. And what did my mom do? She felt so guilty that she went into the closet and pulled out one of her fur coats.

"Mrs. Doyle, I am so sorry. Here you go," my mother draped the coat around Mrs. Doyle's shoulders while my father ushered her to the door.

Yes, my father escorted Mrs. Doyle out into the flying snow and loaded her into her car, urgently directing both my husband and cousin to shovel her out and even help push her over a large snowbank. I can still see Mrs. Doyle, sitting in the driver's seat of the car in the middle of what was now a huge snowstorm, wearing my mom's fur coat. She drove off, fishtailing down the street. And that was the last time we ever saw her.

I used to think that my father was both incredibly brave and incredibly rude in this practice, but, from where I sit now, I see it's sort of a genius, albeit unorthodox, way to reclaim peace of mind, sense of space and, I guess, control over a situation. For someone who loved his Dale Carnegie, my father loved his boundaries more.

So what does this mean for me, his daughter? I wish I had the presence of mind to say similar or at least, say sooner, and also to acknowledge the signs that Ryan clearly saw. The same signs that maybe my father saw? Speaking of signs, this one now hangs outside my house: "You had a very nice time here and you'll be leaving soon."

Colonoscopy
at The Carlyle

It was the Christmas before Covid
and my then-four-year-old daughter Gala
told us that all she wanted from Santa was a
rabbit. We were living in our 14th floor Chelsea apartment at the time so the combination
of missing our beloved beagle Stanley and at
the same time remembering how much we
dreaded walking him in New York City, made
us relieved that she didn't ask for a new dog.

With Christmas two weeks away, I
quickly went online and earned a tiny PhD
in all things Lop Rabbits. A lop rabbit is any
type of rabbit whose ears droop as opposed
to being erect. I learned things like: when do
their ears drop, how long do they live, cage or

free roaming? But the most astonishing fact I learned was that a rabbit poops 200-300 times a day! Crazy, right? But it didn't stop me from saying yes and purchasing a very rare blue bunny from a breeder in southern New Jersey for $150. We named him Spotty Rogers, because he had spots and I love Mr. Rogers.

Rabbits are work. There is zero instant gratification. Unlike dogs who basically love you at first sight, a rabbit's love must be earned. You must first earn their trust. Trust first, love second. So, while Spotty spent the first two weeks hiding from me and wholly terrified of our daughter, I spent much of that time on the floor, watching Amy Sedaris Rabbit Care videos and waiting patiently for him to begin to trust me. Little by little he did. Spotty became mine.

This wasn't my first rabbit. When I was ten years old, I had a rabbit named Bunny (I know, I know, that's like naming your dog Bark) that a kind lawn worker found digging up our yard and handed over to me. He was tiny, scared and abandoned by his mother. I was delighted to "Save Bunny" and my mother was wonderful to oblige by taking me and Bunny to the vet to get a special formula that I would feed to him ten times a day with an eye dropper. Bunny lived for two whole days under my care and when he died I listened to Whitney Houston's "All At Once" on repeat for a month, crying my eyes out for Bunny each time Whitney hit that high C.

Now here I am almost thirty-five years later, a rabbit mama again, after a year of pure and total rabbit obsession. Spotty would do yoga with me, sit at my feet while I wrote, bite my hand violently to signal it was time to get neutered (leaving a helluva lover's scar) and eventually even quarantining with us. He watched me cook in the kitchen and tried to eat our popcorn from the bowl as we watched movies on the couch. Then Christmas was upon us again and Spotty, now over one year old, "binked" with joy around our tree as we decorated, sang holiday songs and wrapped presents. "Binking" is what you call it when a rabbit is so happy that they hop in the air and twist around, like a special kind of happy dance. It's really quite joyful to watch.

That Christmas Eve, while hosting the family, Ryan and I generously helped ourselves to a martini or two or maybe three. What's left in the shaker doesn't count, right? My mother, sister and I launched into our annual Christmas danceathon and singalong, so funny I deemed it Insta-postable. A perfect, happy, joyful Christmas Eve.

And then . . . .

There was suddenly the most horrific sound I have ever heard reverberate through the house. My sister's dog Lola, who was secured outside, accidentally got into the house and attacked Spotty. Rabbits are prey to most dogs. I just wasn't thinking when all of the kids asked if the dog could come inside "if we watch him." At the time, I wanted to say, "No," but I didn't. I did what I always did. I tried to accommodate everyone; tried to make everyone happy, judgment impaired by too many martinis. What followed next were screams, tears, and frantic calls to try to find a rabbit vet on Christmas Eve. Ryan and my brother-in-law finally drove in the pouring rain to Nanuet Animal Hospital, about two hours away—the only Urgent Care that would see rabbits on Christmas Eve.

At 5 am, Ryan returned home with Spotty, barely alive, with a wrapped front paw and a small plastic cone around his listless head, I cared for him all of Christmas Day, feeding him water from an eye dropper (just like I had with Bunny), tried to get him to eat, and attempted to warm his shivering body. The next day, I found a rabbit "expert" in the city and wrapped Spotty in the coziest blanket in the house, placed him in a box on the passenger seat of my car and for two hours rubbed his ears with one hand while steering with the other until I placed him in the care of the skilled vet.

To some, this would just be seen as one of these crazy animal stories told years later around a dinner table; the Christmas Eve the rabbit died—yes, sadly he did. Even this skilled vet couldn't save him. But this whole event represented so much more to me.

You see, while I was crossing the George Washington Bridge, rubbing Spotty's ears and praying for him to survive, I sent out a message to God, the Universe, the Ghost of the GW Bridge (is there a Ghost of the GW Bridge?), any talisman or icon that would listen. In reflection, I was asking someone or something to get a message to me.

And that message?

I needed to get control of my life. I needed to stop trying to please everyone all of the time (hard, yes, for an event planner). I needed to stop the excess of Covid lockdown and let's face it, the twenty-seven years of legendary good times prior to that. I needed to get to the root of why I was so good at caring for others and so bad at caring for myself.

Right on target, the week after Spotty died, came that magic moment when we all seemed to start remerging from Covid isolation (with a few extra pounds, more gray hairs than we'd like and lots of uncleaned teeth). It was also precisely the time my body's dashboard "check liver" light was flashing boldly. I realized that it was time to get a checkup (both mental and physical) before all my "check engine" lights went off at once.

"You need a colonoscopy, and you need to get it this week." My fellow Hoya doctor, a tall handsome man in his mid to late seventies (who looked like a character actor), who still smoked in between patients and poured himself a scotch while delivering both good and bad news across the large desk covered with medical journals was now telling me I had to have my "pooper" checked. Ok, for the record, he did not use the word "pooper."

And while we usually banter at these appointments about our old Georgetown Alma Mater, there was a sternness in his tone that alerted me that I had to take my tush in for an inspection, pronto.

We had relocated to Woodstock during Covid and subleased our Chelsea apartment to our neighbors so I did not have a city abode in which to stay for the next two days to prepare for my rump's television debut. So I thought, "Hmmm, where could I go that would ease my anxiety, allow me a comfortable place to prepare my digestive tract and take my brain off what could potentially be some really bad news based on my symptoms?"

First choice . . . The Carlyle Hotel. It was blocks away from both my doctor and where I would be having my procedure and it had been a bit of a dream to stay there my whole life.

A bastion of Upper East Side sophistication known for impeccable service and privacy, The Carlyle Hotel has captivated the world's most sophisticated travelers since its debut in 1930.
—The Carlyle Hotel website

Known for its "strong commitment to excellence" in the quality of both service and discretion, I quickly deduced that if it was good enough for Jackie O, Princess Diana, Michael Jackson, JFK and Marilyn Monroe, then it was certainly going to be good enough for me.

I was also lucky that this was still Covid times so the normally outside my budget rooms were now discounted as the famous Bemelmans's Bar and Café Carlyle were still shut down. This was bad news to many, but great news to me, as I would then not be tempted to sneak in a perfectly chilled martini from downstairs in between my bowel prep cocktails.

"I'll be staying at The Carlyle for the next two days," I informed Ryan who could hear in my voice that this decision was as non-refundable as my room. He told me to try to relax and not let my brain travel to where it usually goes—death. I planned to enjoy it the best I could, reminding myself of the million thread count sheets, the silence of being away from my husband and daughter (first time in over a year) and all the movies I could devour.

Once I arrived and stepped into the hotel lobby I was gobsmacked, as I was suddenly surrounded by rabbits. Rabbits everywhere the eye could see. First, the incredible black and white lobby artwork by Rudolf Stingel that are based on famed *Madeline* children's author and illustrator Ludwig Bemelmans rabbits that adorn the walls of the cafe a room away. There's a rabbit dressed in a three-piece suit smoking a cigar and a group of equally sophisticated rabbits enjoying an ornate party. In the cafe are the murals of rabbits enjoying an outdoor luncheon and strolling with parasols. Once in my room, I find more rabbits, including a beautiful silver one contained inside the glass base of an ornate bed lamp, perfectly placed on the same side of the bed where I prefer to sleep.

I felt myself swinging back and forth between the little girl saving the abandoned bunny and the mother salvaging her daughter's mistaken new pet. Who was I really kidding, Spotty had always been mine.

And as I swayed in place with these memories, I almost didn't hear the bellman tell me that all I had to do was call the front desk and they would bring me anything I wanted. I once read an article on "the most bizarre yet granted hotel requests" which included: framed photos of Jeff Goldblum, a bathtub filled with wild oat milk and an adult sized pillow fort. I knew I was definitely in a place that could grant all of those wishes and more. Once the bellman left, I finished playing "hotel," by taking in all the remaining details of the beautiful room, and the view that revealed a perfect slice of Central Park. I was most definitely in love.

But I wasn't there to attend the Met Ball across the street or meet Bill Murray for duets at the bar *a la* Sofia Coppola. I was there to eliminate the entire contents of me prior to a medical procedure. So it was time for me to get intimate with the bathroom, a beautiful porcelain bowl and marble bathtub with pretty glass bottles of fabulous soaps and lotions. I'll spare you the gory details but for all you first timers out there: compostable, flushable baby wipes (lots of them), Vaseline and access to a bathtub. The next day, it was like I'd lost twenty pounds, which, after almost two years of Covid bacchanal, felt great.

Naturally, in the middle of the night, I woke up starving and tempted by the most extravagant mini-bar in the world: José Andres potato chips, Peanut M&M's in glass jars, vodka of all types. I resisted by looking out the window at the sliver of moon hanging over Central Park and delighted that New York was still here, resilient, magical. How many people staying in this exact room, looking at this exact view, had their breath taken away by the possibilities that make up this city?

New York City had granted my wishes and dreams, reminding me of one of my favorite childhood books, *The Giving Tree*. I arrived here in 1997 and just gobbled it all up, literally and figuratively and now I stood here, intentionally hungry for more. But had I treated New York City like the boy treated the tree?

Had I taken too much? Was this payback time? I guess I'd soon find out when I sat at the desk across from Dr. Fellow Alumni.

After first placing a chair firmly in front of the mini bar, I fell back into the cloudlike bed and attempted to sleep, wondering when I'd get woozy enough to drift off and just how many rabbits lived on the walls, in the frames and in the furniture of this wonderful building, The Carlyle Hotel. I wondered if anyone had ever thought to count. So I began . . . counting rabbits.

Bees Sleep
in Flowers

How to lose friends and influence no one is the polar opposite of how I have spent more than half my life. To know me is to know I always play nice, crave the love of everybody around me, do what is expected and deliver that in a bankable, relatable brand to make my family and colleagues proud. This in turn has created my character, perhaps caricature, of my own life. And I was ready to toss it all away.

In the midst of this revelation, I realized that I had no idea how to exorcise this Mary, or if I would even be granted "permission" from all those who relied on me in one way or another to do so. But I did recall that some of the happiest moments of my life have been when I have allowed myself to get lost in the freedom of forgetting who I was. No more daughter, sister, wife, mother. No more caterer to the stars. And certainly no more, "Wait, what? Giuliani?"

"I don't know who I am or what I want anymore," I told my friend Pearl. "I can't look at my phone for another minute, watching other people live their lives or pretend to live their lives. I need to make sure my brain still works. That I can still write."

I confessed this to Pearl on the same call where I was hoping to convince her to travel from California to the Catskills to attend a week-long writing workshop with me. One full week of surrender in the woods without husbands or kids, without emails from work or school. No pressure to be anyone or anything. Nothing to do, and no place to go except wherever my notebook took me.

I found this trip literally at the eleventh hour, after I had Googled "writing workshops" and saw this intensive session "Memoir As Bewilderment," being offered by Nick Flynn. Here's the definition of bewilderment: "a feeling of being perplexed and confused." I was a hundred percent in. But I just needed to convince Pearl that she was as perplexed and confused as I was.

We knew very little about our writing instructor other than he was a respected writer whose brave memoir, *Another Bullshit Night in Suck City,* we had both read and had wholly agreed with its rave reviews, not to mention that it features one of the best titles ever. Plus he was married to one of our favorite 1980s movie stars, Lili Taylor, whose character Corey famously sang the ballad "Joe Lies (When He Cries)" in the movie *Say Anything.* Naturally, it was nearly impossible for Pearl and I to stop singing that in our heads on our way to class for the first few days.

I was beyond elated when Pearl agreed to join me and we headed straight from the airport to Target to get matching retreat gear: comfy sweats, slippers, eye masks, and (the best part) school supplies. We were given a list: notebooks, pencils, folders, scissors, glue, and tape. It made us giddy, two forty-six-year olds purchasing school supplies for . . . ourselves!

One hour later Pearl and I arrived at the dharma-like campus in the middle of the woods. We checked into our side-by-side cabins that were very sparse: a simple desk, bed, and bathroom—no distractions. It was perfect for me and my never-fully-tuned-down brain. After the excess of the previous year, the simplicity of all this completely appealed to me. There was very little to maintain, clean, take care of other than putting the cap back on the toothpaste and, maybe if I felt like it, make the bed.

I felt like I was living out my childhood dream of attending sleepaway camp, which I was forbidden to do as a child, since my mother deemed sleepaway camp, "a place where parents who don't love their children send them for the summer so they can drink and 'take pot.'" My mother has never taken or smoked pot.

My father also told me at an early age, "Mary, there are beach people and there are mountain people, and we are beach people." Well, turns out I was in fact a mountain person. Taking in the fresh air and stillness outside my cabin felt like life support.

Pearl and I met on the front porch each morning to walk to class. We'd stroll past a food hall straight out of *Dirty Dancing* that always seemed to smell like a meal in progress, but never actually inspired hunger as the aromas were a combo of hospital soup mixed with patchouli.

That first morning we passed a quiet woman who was intensely staring at a clump of flowers.

"You know, bees sleep in flowers," she said to us as we came upon her. She then turned and continued conversing with her new pollinator friends. Oddly compelled, we also looked down, and yes, she was right. "I'm Cathy," she said, falling in step with us on the approach to the writing room, as we became fast friends.

It's so funny to go "to school" with friends you make when you're older. You automatically assume your high school roles: I was the funny one, immediately settling back into my comedic stride; Pearl was the pretty, mysterious, artistic one, walking slowly, always one step behind us; and Cathy was the studious thoughtful one, blurting out certain facts about the property as we walked along, like how the retreat was founded by an Eastern scholar, a holistic medical doctor and an educator in 1977, two years after Pearl and I were born.

Because of the sleeping bees, we were late and while I pride myself on promptness, I was not too hard on myself this time. I was too overjoyed to walk into a room where no one knew me or knew what I did for a living or, most importantly, weren't able to quick-judge my last name.

Nick had placed twenty envelopes on a table in front of the classroom and on each envelope he had written two simple words and a symbol. He instructed us to go up and grab one that spoke to us. Since we were late, there were only two envelopes left, so I walked to the front of the room and picked up the lone envelope after Pearl grabbed hers first. The outside of mine read, "To Forget" and ironically had a spoon as the symbol next to it.

Nick asked everyone to go around the room, say their name and read the words on their envelope out loud. This roll call commenced, everyone using their first names, "Tim, to love. "Joyce, to give." When it gets to my turn, I am so excited to be just Mary for a whole week, so I begin . . . "Mary—"

"Wait!" Nick interrupted. "What's your last name? There are two Marys in class this week."

Damnit!

I began to sweat and turned red. I came here literally to forget and now I was the only person in the class being asked to confess immediately who I was. I know that every time I say my last name out loud in public, it's either knowing smiles and even thumb's up. Or usually and even worse, I get the opposite: grunts, grimaces, and possibly even rage. I knew how workshops work. That's the beauty of them. You get to be raw and unfiltered and if classmates hated my writing style or critiqued my dialogue with daggers, fine. But I did not want to begin this week with strangers who were going to be instantly swayed not by my language but by my last name. I simply could not start the workshop this way, I thought over and over in that moment. Suddenly, I realized what I had to do.

"Okay. Mary G., to forget" Crisis averted, and I remained just Mary G. for the rest of the retreat.

Now the only thing I had to focus on were the words to forget and my symbol, the spoon.

So I took my symbol literally. I was ready to stir my own pot, to mix out the Mary I had steadfastly been for everyone else and mix in Mary G.—who? I didn't know yet. All I knew was that I was ready to meet her.

On the last night of the retreat, I called home to Ryan, who asked, "how's it going?" I told him that the workshop was wonderful, that I had written a lot and that I was excited to share it all with him but warned him that the material was, "a little dark," not realizing that I was on speaker, and that my daughter, with that perfect six-year-old rational mind, would pipe up to ask, "Mommy, don't they have a lamp in your cabin?"

After a good laugh, I hung up, walked out onto the small porch, and turned on the outside light, realizing that while I was happy to be Mary G. here in my writer's cocoon, uncovering this and that, I was so grateful and excited to return home to being Mary, mother, wife, and also writer.

Hello! My Name is Mary—Not Mayor

mary giuliani

Q All   Images   News   Videos   Shopping   More

About 4,350,000 results (0.58 seconds)

People also ask

Is Mary Giuliani Rudy's daughter?   ˅

Who is Mary Giuliani husband?   ˅

Feedback

Imagine landing in New York City over twenty-five years ago with five hundred dollars and zero connections; working your tiny Sicilian tail off; growing a business from scratch that has been recognized with both an impressive client roster and earning a few awards and industry praise along the way; appearing on television on a fairly regular basis as an "expert party planner;" writing not one, not two but three books . . . and . . . the majority of people Googling me only have one burning question: "Is Mary Giuliani related to Rudy Giuliani?"

But wait! There's more!
• On my office voicemail, an enthusiastic message from a supportive Rudy fan greets me when I check my inbox, imploring me to tell "your father" to run for President.
• A box of cigars presented to me at an event to give to my "dad."
• A charity event: I donated the food and drink to the sponsoring organization. I am introduced to the VIP celeb performer (an 80s pop star who is known for championing many of the same democratic causes I also heartily support) and I watch her face shift and morph into not only puzzlement, but outright disdain. It's only after my publicist whispers in her ear that I'm not "that kind of Giuliani" does VIP celeb deign to speak to me.

Greatest diss of all?
At a doctor's appointment, where I sat naked, shivering, and petrified, fervently prayed to my guardian angels (grandmothers Mary and Lucille and my beloved pal Lee Blumer), as

I waited to be brought in for a full body scan in order to determine if I had . . . multi-organ cancer. Yes, multi-organ cancer, I overheard the nurse and the doctor, outside the exam room, looking over my chart and whispering "Giuliani?" "Hope she's not related." Ok, so the good news . . . I don't have cancer. But the bad news? On top of every horrible scenario that was running through my mind as I sat there in that thin pink gown and fuzzy socks, their disdainful whispers are the straw that broke the proverbial camel's back.

Then there's this

"I'd never buy that book." A white haired woman in her sixties stage-whispers to her pal, scowling at me with her eyes narrowed and nose scrunched in outrage, as I sit in my chair at the East Hampton Book Fair as an invited author there to sign copies of my books to people who ostensibly are excited to read me. That look of pure disdain? Not because we chatted, and she thought I was an idiot. Nope. She just saw my last name on my books and assumed she knew my story.

My story

Let's start with the basic question. Am I related? The answer is yes-ish. When I was twenty-two, I fell in love with a distant cousin of Rudy's, my husband Ryan. At twenty-five, we got married and since I adored both Ryan and his immediate family, especially his grandma Evelyn and her stuffed artichokes, I joyfully took both his hand in marriage and his last name. But when I say that Ryan is a distant cousin and people ask, just how distant? I am quick to state the below facts; I've had more conversations with Robert DeNiro and Mick Jagger than I've ever had with Rudy Giuliani. I have never catered a party for him and have gone out of my way to distinguish myself as "not that Giuliani" by wearing both a Giuliani for Clinton AND a Giuliani for Biden t-shirt during the last two elections, rounding out my anti-Giuliani wardrobe in my very fancy Lingua Franca sweater that I had custom made during my last book tour that announces in embroidery, "It's Mary NOT Mayor."

More facts: I wasn't a fan of Rudy Giuliani far before it was cool to despise him. Mainy because he got rid of all the things I loved about Old New York (Separately, Google "Murray Hill runs against Giuliani for Mayor" because had I been in residence in New York City at that time, my pal Murray would have had my vote, as well as my time campaigning and I certainly would have thrown him an election night party, the likes of which this town had never seen). Giuliani closed the dirty New York nudie bars, the after-hour nightclubs, the gay bars, the dancing, the smoking (hmm, maybe that was Bloomberg?), the artists, the dreamers. That was my fantasy New York and these people, they were the New Yorkers that in my eyes made New York, well, New York. That was the New York I hoped to someday call home, after escaping the Island of Long. I wanted to live, breathe, and ...and create a life for myself amidst "my people" in the dark watering holes and nightclubs of that now bygone era.

So in January of 2015, I got my chance to actually DO something about my fantasy verison of NYC, the one I thought I missed out on living, when I received a call from one of my favorite and most powerful clients—that's quite a combo, so when my phone lights up with his name, no matter where I am, no matter who I'm with, I take his call. On this occasion, this particular call came in while Ryan and I were at a Chuck E. Cheese down South, entertaining the surrogate carrying our soon-to-be-born daughter and her family. Walking away from the blaring music of the Munch's Make Believe Band, an animatronic band that has successfully been playing at Chuck E. Cheese's restaurants since 1989, I answered the call and true to form, my client got right down to business. No "hello"—just go!

"Do you know who (let's call him) Mr. X is?"

"The real estate Mr. X? Yes, yes I do."

"Good. He's calling you in ten minutes."

Confused but also intrigued, I excused myself from the next round of Skee Ball and stepped outside into the parking lot of the Chuck E. Cheese to await the call from this real estate magnate, possibly the one with the most chutzpah in the game right now. This was clearly a big deal.

The phone rang. "Who are you?" is the first thing I hear, upon answering my own phone. Chutzpah up the wazoo.

Days after our ten minute chat in that parking lot, I found myself in a Masters of the Universe executive suite overlooking Central Park, being asked if I could introduce better food experiences into a neighborhood notorious for truly dismal dining: Midtown West. This no-man's zone, the area that surrounds Madison Square Garden heading towards the Hudson River, seemed like the last frontier. I immediately loved the idea of pioneering these streets. It felt like Old New York. My Fantasy New York. Hooray and hell yes! I was IN!

For the next few weeks, I traipsed up and down the streets and avenues of some of the dirtiest corners of the city. This was totally full circle for me. Penn Station was my entry point, when I was daytripping into the city as a little girl, fantasizing about my future life here while holding my mother's hand for dear life. These surroundings were precisely the New York that greeted me when I stepped foot in the city, so it was almost surreal to think I might have a hand in reimagining what might come next. Armed with a map of the neighborhood, I nosed around abandoned buildings, partial construction sites and came across what I am sure were one or two murder scenes.

In the end, I stood up in front of a room of twenty-plus executives, mostly men in suits, and declared, "This city is too clean, too commercial, and it shows. Too many artists, or even artistic types, can't call it home or even try to make it here anymore. If you want me to head up this 'rebirth,' as we're calling it, I want to be known as the Giuliani who makes the city 'dirty' again, but by that I mean we need the creatives to come back, and we must make rents and spaces affordable for them," urging them to turn the rotting Pennsylvania Hotel (also the inspiration for Glenn Miller's "Pennsylvania 6-5000") into affordable artist lofts.

I continued, "That goes ditto for restaurants, which are decamping to the outer boroughs. Your neighborhood is already a shithole and if you want new restaurants, new blood, new energy on the streets, I'm your girl. I want to help keep the fork in New York."

Part of me thought they'd laugh me out of the room but Mr. X, perhaps impressed with my chutzpah, handed me a map of the neighborhood and a pen asked me to "pick the buildings you want." Imagine getting handed a map of New York City to cherry-pick from it what you wanted?

As all eyes in the boardroom were on me, the obvious grab on the map would have been the corner of 7th Avenue and 33rd, an abandoned Borders bookstore, where we eventually did open The Pennsy food hall. But that wasn't the space that initially grabbed me. It was way too obvious. Nope, it was a shipping dock on 33rd and 9th, as well as an above-ground glass bridge that connected 33rd to 32nd Street. But my favorite thing on the map? An underground area of Seventh Avenue known as the Gimbels Corridor. Now, that REALLY got my attention! I devoted more time, now underground, exploring this dirty tunnel, a place Jimmy Breslin described this way in a November 28, 2010, *New York Post* article:

"To revisit the long-closed Gimbels Corridor is to relive New York's past-tense future. In the early 1970s, conditions in the pedestrian tunnel presaged the bleeding city of the 1980s and early '90s. Filthy, fetid and unpoliced, it entertained rampant lawlessness, squalor and decay years before they fully possessed the streets."

I became obsessed with this tunnel and tried with all my might to share this excitement with anyone brave enough to dirty their fancy shoes with grit, asbestos or what I started to proudly point out on my tours as "real blood."

I took titans of industry, famous architects, Broadway producers on a tour to share what I was now calling, "the greatest hidden gem of New York City," a place that stirs the soul to abandon all logic and reason and propels you to think BIG.

So . . . did I make a convincing argument? Not really.

I was able to launch one project that felt authentic to my vision, a food truck "incubator" located in an old shipping and receiving dock on 33rd Street that I aptly named Shipping & Receiving. I launched my first Eating Stories event—think The Moth but with food—at that loading dock in 2015 in conjunction with The New York Wine and Food Festival, which felt like a real triumph. While a success, The Pennsy wasn't really part of my original vision at all, teaching me the lesson that the shiny penny (or Pennsy) is not always the better coin. Sadly, I never got anyone past their squeamishness about The Gimbels Corridor. Win some, lose some.

And yet, here I sit today, still Googling away and seeing again and again: "Is Mary Giuliani related to Rudy Giuliani?" After all that, all those miles logged in the Gimbels Corridor, coming home and leaving my shoes outside of my apartment so as not to track asbestos into my house and literally staying up night after night, imagining the incredible changes I could have inspired, had those executives shared my vision, to say nothing of the opening night parties!

So . . . back to this last name. Am I going to allow my blood pressure to rise every time I get a Google alert about Rudy? Am I going to let the old lady at the East Hampton Book Fair, who will no doubt be there again this year, once again ruffle my feathers when she gives me another dirty look just upon seeing my name?

Nah, I'm going to go on living my life as just Mary. Loving me or hating me instantly simply by hearing my last name is now your choice and no longer my problem. Placing me in a box without knowing my whole story is your right entirely but that right will no longer be my burden. My job is to keep doing the things that make me stand out. I've even set a new fun goal that someday, the number one thing that comes up when Rudy Giuliani Googles himself will be, "Is Rudy Giuliani related to Mary Giuliani?"

Smoking With Celebrities

"You smell like two things I love. Tequila and cigarettes."

This was a "true confession" from a very bold-faced celebrity, whom I grew up idolizing on television.

"Meet me in the bushes in ten minutes with both?"

I should note, she was wearing a wedding gown and I was catering her special day on a donkey farm. And while this sounds unlikely, both a wedding on a donkey farm and catering your childhood imaginary best friend's wedding, this type of stuff happens to me . . . a lot.

"Wait, Mary smokes?"

The answer is "No!" if the person asking is my parents, parents' friends, my in-laws, or my daughter. To everyone else, yes Mary sometimes smokes, but I am proud to say that I have greatly reduced my smoking habit—the habit of which I once boasted as being "so good that if smoking was an Olympic sport, I'd win a medal!" Since the birth of my child, I now reserve this treasured ritual for only stressful events and only with celebrities.

People assume it's glamorous that I work with celebrities. They also assume that I am friends with them, but the truth is, most of the time I've never even met the bold-faced celebs I'm hired to feed, as I mostly work with "their people." My pigs in a blanket may get me in the room, but my cigarette habit is what often gets me the real face time. I've found smoking to be as intimate as sharing a secret, a confession, an act after a sexual encounter. An occasion that is often magical, well, at least for me.

In the beginning, I took these divine nicotine meetings as some sort of mystical, cosmic fate. Here's the math:

Mary

+ right place
+ right time

+ pack of cigarettes
+ meeting behind the kitchen or garage
 where caterers work

= magical encounters with all my heroes
= new best friendships

The disappointing truth is that each of these encounters only lasted for the amount of time it took from lit tip to filter, or, if I was lucky, two. And no matter how much we shared over embers; when it was over we dropped it to the ground and twisted it out with our heels as we each turned to go our separate ways.

I once made the terrible miscalculation, three cigarettes in, that Drew Barrymore and I were going to be best friends. We bonded over the fact that we were the same age, both moms, both producers (me of events, she of her eponymously named talk show), positive energies, lovers of life and that nothing was better than the smell of the Atlantic Ocean air mixing with gardenias in the summer. She said things like, "We will meet again," and "This was meant to be." I even got dangerously close to confessing to her that I enjoyed my burgeoning childhood sexuality by masturbating on my ET doll's face.

Thank God I didn't.

The next week, I was heartbroken when I went in for an embrace at another event as Drew blank-stared her way right past me toward my taco bar. Maybe she quit? Oh, when will I ever learn?

This was when I realized that all my cigarette packs should come not only with, yes, the Surgeon General's warning, but also with a direct quote from one of my favorite characters of all time, Lester Bangs in *Almost Famous*, played by the amazing Phillip Seymour Hoffman. Bangs warns the film's young star-struck protagonist before he's about to go on the road with his favorite band: "These are not your friends."

Don't feel too sad for me, because while these fine folks of stage and screen didn't exactly invite me to Cabo after these chance encounters, I am proud to say that I've smoked with some of the best . . . .

And if I were to list all the people that work in food who also smoke, then we'd have to add a few more chapters. I think the combination of stress, lots of downtime and the fact that most people who work in food are self-proclaimed rebels, makes smoking an attractive accessory. When chefs graduate from culinary school, their diplomas should come with a pack of Marlboros.

So I have an impressive resumé of celebrities with whom I've smoked. But is it truly all-star? Let's change up that parlor game, rephrase the late night talk show question. Forget the proposed dinner party you'd have with the five historical figures of all time. How about the five most famous people of all time with whom I would love to sit on a fire escape in January, passing around the lighter:

In no particular order: Nora Ephron, Toni Morrison, Sophia Loren, Jackie Gleason, my Papa Charlie.

And lest we forget, the Mothership of all smokers: Fran Leibowitz. But let's save that for another chapter . . .

Send in
the Clowns

For years I would listen to this song and think about my grandparents Franklin and Lucille, for Stephen Sondheim perfectly describes the demise of their marriage in just a few simple lyrics. Their marriage arc played like a movie. A piano teacher from Queens and an engineer who worked in a public school go on to create a successful hotel empire in the sleepy, but soon-to-be up-and-coming beach town of Montauk, New York. They achieved success beyond their wildest dreams: fancy parties, ribbon cuttings, expensive cars, new friends from faraway places—the works.

I spent the first ten summers of my life at

71

my grandmother's crowning achievement, The Wavecrest Resort, six acres of land on the Atlantic Ocean, seventy oceanfront rooms, an indoor swimming pool, shuffleboard courts, and a snack shack with all the hot dogs and French fries that my little body could gobble. It was always referred to as "your grandmother's resort," as she was the force of nature behind it all. She was also president of the chamber of commerce. She opened the first medical center in town. She built her first hotel in town in the shape of an "L" for the first letter of her name. She even astutely bought the ferry rights from Montauk to Block Island. She hosted wild parties with an assortment of eclectic friends. Growing up it was always "she," "she," "she"—Lucille.

My grandparents divorced before I was born so, I knew very little about my grandfather other than that he left behind a small boat at the hotel. It was dry-docked on land in between two of the large buildings that housed most of the guest rooms. When we would pass the boat on the way down to the beach, my father would always say, "That was your grandfather's. He loved to fish. He's a good man." But that was it. The only image I had of Franklin was a boat without water.

The "tipping point" story of their demise,

was that one night at the height of their success, at one of her lavish parties, Franklin took Lucille onto the balcony of their home that overlooked the oceanfront resort that he helped build with his hands. They looked down at the cars lined up and down the resort's driveway, and the Atlantic's waves crashing onto the beach, and he said something like: "Lucille, I gave you the best years of my life. I never wanted all of this. I can't do this anymore. I'm leaving." He returned to their simple home in Queens, near Kennedy Airport, leaving Lucille behind in the remnants of the business they spent most of their marriage building.

If that weren't dramatic enough, Lucille eventually died alone, surrounded by stacks of romance novels on her bedside table and "friends," if your definition of friends is freeloaders, drunks and strangers, looking to live off someone else's fame and fortune.

How and when did it all go wrong? Their story for me never went beyond the one I was told, distilled into its simplest form. She wanted more, he wanted less. The divorce was messy. She died alone.

I never delved deeper into their sad history until one day, in my mid-forties, when I was driving to our house upstate and "Send in the Clowns" came on the radio. That was the day I realized that I was no longer associating the song lyrics to Franklin and Lucille. It was now about me and my marriage to Ryan.

Ryan and I met the summer I graduated college. Prior to Ryan, I had two long term relationships, one in high school and one in college. My college boyfriend was perfect. A wonderful, smart, handsome, athletic, kind, really going places kind of gentleman. It seems silly now, but when we graduated, we decided to spend a summer apart as I was sure we would soon get engaged. I planned on being a Mrs. to his Mr., pursue an acting career, but really just bide my time until I was a mother. He'd go to work, and I'd stay home with the kids, a devoted wife and parent. Yes, it was all painfully old-fashioned, but at the time that seemed like a no-brainer to anyone who knew my family.

I went out to Montauk to have one last summer of independence before becoming a wife. I moved in with my family, who had just finished building their dream house a few miles down the road from Grandma Lucille's hotel. It was the first time we were in our own home as opposed to a summer rental or the cottage we still owned on the property at The Wavecrest. I got a job at The Farmhouse, a restaurant in Amagansett, because I knew if I was going to move to New York in September to pursue my acting career, I should get used to working in restaurants. But really, I chose to work there because back in the day it was called The Spring Close House where my Grandmother Lucille used to reign as queen, as it was still the place to see and be seen.

As the hostess, I worked long days and nights. And unlike the other girls my age who were out every night at trendy clubs like Jet East and The Tavern, I went home to my parents after work, watching movies or playing board games. With my future husband across the country for the summer, I had zero interest in hookups or a sloppy bar scene.

Everything was indeed going to plan until Ryan, fresh from a ten-hour drive from his college in Virginia to a bartending job at The Farmhouse, walked through the restaurant's front door. He had long hair and a Phish T-shirt (my least favorite band ever), but that didn't stop me from seeing stars in his beautiful hazel eyes. In a sentence, my life trajectory was forever changed. I can't explain the feeling as I'd never felt it before and have never felt it since, but our first exchange, a simple hello, felt deliciously heavy, like the molecular structure of the universe had shifted.

Jump ahead through many, many conversations between us, me at the hostess stand, him behind the bar, and I knew in my heart that my plan to marry the perfect college boyfriend was over. Not for the reason he did anything wrong or that I didn't love him. I felt life with him would be easy but to be honest, I was tired of everything in my life being so easy. And this new life I was imagining with Ryan while showing people to their tables? Definitely not cushy, in fact, without a lot of glamor or even decent furniture. A crumbling apartment in the village, if we could afford the rent. Some wild artistic friends, and besides my own acting bug, Ryan was a pretty great fledgling photographer with ambitions of his own. Nothing about this imagined life would come easy but that didn't matter. I was smitten with Ryan and the idea of this new me as half of a new us.

When our summer of love ended, we packed up and headed to New York City to chase our dreams. Those early days were exactly what I had hoped: exciting, with the promise of a deepening love. As I was in the West Village and Ryan in the East, paying two rents when we spent nearly every night together seemed crazy. On a snowy Christmas Eve on the Bow Bridge in Central Park, Ryan dropped to his knee and asked me to marry him. We were still, in the words of Patti Smith, "just kids."

Our wedding in Montauk was beautiful, our honeymoon filled with lots of gelato, prosecco, sex, and swimming in Positano. When we returned, we placed our wedding gifts onto our shelves and laughed. "Do you even know what to do with a food processor?"

But something had changed in me. It was as if the wedding ring on my finger altered my DNA. I was no longer footloose, artistic, free. After years of dream chasing but never catching, it was time to think about our future. We were a married couple with a new fancy blender and a high-tech coffeemaker, and it was time for us to grow up, accept the responsibilities that married life brings: get real jobs before the kids came.

While Ryan hung up his camera for a suit and a desk at an ad agency, I accepted the realization that I would not be the next Gilda Radner. I took a job at a catering company where I pushed myself to the limits, the hardest I ever worked in my life. While working for someone else's catering company, we realized that I had what it takes to run my own. And since Ryan was growing more and more allergic to anything corporate America, we decided to take a leap of faith together, and that's how Mary Giuliani Catering & Events was born.

We handmade our business cards on which I glued tiny little artichokes, and we dreamed up fun, playful party food ideas while Ryan set up all the business systems we would need. Ryan felt strongly we should name the company Mary Giuliani since I was the happy hostess with all the great ideas for party planning perfection. What could go wrong?

In a word . . . everything.

Our business did enjoy an almost immediate blush of success, but the lines between "husband and wife" and "business partner and business partner," got blurry and then downright sloppy. There was resentment on both sides as both our dreams got shelved and traditional gender roles reversed. I had grown up in a house where my father provided everything for "his girls." Day after day, he kissed us goodbye, left for work, came home for dinner, woke up and did it again. The idea of my mother staying out until all hours of the night working, schmoozing with clients, drinking, and smoking with staff and celebs alike, while my father stayed home? That made no sense to me and yet, that's what happened. My life with Ryan in no way resembled the marriage model with which I was raised, and it was starting to make me angry.

I started referring to it as my catering company, instead of our catering company, even though Ryan truly kept the business working behind the scenes, I was furious that I always had to be the "face" of the business. I was the one working the battlefield of buffets, night after night.

And not only was I resentful at this weird switch of our roles, I was also surprised to find I had become hungry, in fact, starved, for attention and recognition. If I was going to have to party-hop my way through thirty-some events during New York Fashion Week, I wanted a television crew there to follow my every move.

I began taking meetings for the multiple reality show pitches I received monthly. "Mary, we'd love to follow you and your husband around and film all the hijinks. Could we get a few famous faces on screen too, preferably behaving badly?" Um, no. For every decent idea pitched to me about a show revolving around the life of Mary, "Caterer To The Stars," there were incessant requests for me to throw fits (even chairs) and generally behave like an asshole. I turned them all down saying, "We don't have that type of drama at our events." I didn't share that I saved all the yelling and table tossing for my time at home with Ryan.

I don't want to make it seem like this newborn, hurling-towards-the-top business was a mistake. It wasn't. We did beautiful things together, threw exciting events, met wonderful, warm people who we still consider to be among our closest friends. There's real pride in what we built and what continues to thrive. I just came to the harsh realization that two people simply cannot share the same dream.

And, like Lucille and Franklin, we found ourselves dangerously close to making the trip to that balcony overlooking a stormy Atlantic.

Ryan had been slowly pulling himself out of the business. He showed up at fewer and fewer parties, was quieter in staff meetings, and more short-tempered with me. In a way, he was morphing into his own form of monster, but while mine was hogging the limelight, he was battling with himself, trying to figure out what would motivate him to get out of bed in the morning. It wasn't going to be a suit and corporate career, and it certainly wasn't a new ways to present pigs in a blanket. The guy who said we should name our company after me was sick of the whole thing—just as I was starting to think we were getting sick of each other.

"We have to choose between us or the business. We can't have both," I said many times, more and more angry that it seemed to fall on deaf ears. It wasn't until Ryan decided on his next move, carving out a stake in the up-and-coming Hudson Valley hospitality movement, that he agreed I was correct.

But this was not the quick fix for which I was hoping, because as Ryan began to move away from what we built together into something on his own, my whole "cake and eat it too" ego came out guns blazing. How could he have success without me? Would he still need me as much? I needed him needing me.

We fought louder and harder than ever before, saying things that are hard to take back. We learned how to live without each other, and grew more and more comfortable in the moments apart. Knee deep in construction, we went deep into debt and put everything we had on the line for what I called "his business." He was getting slammed almost weekly by local planning boards, and then came home to me who would be there to yell at him louder. I never asked him but, I always thought that he must have felt a lot like *Goodfellas* character, Henry Hill, when he arrives late to wife Karen's parents home and before he even steps through the door, Karen and her mother start screaming at him. The scene is relatable, laughable and very scary.

At this point "Send In The Clowns" came on the radio, and I realized that if we kept this up, we too would become a cautionary story for our own grandchildren to tell while they walked around Woodstock Way, Ryan's new hotel property. I could clearly imagine them discussing how their grandparents had achieved so much, but how it ultimately destroyed them.

That was a sobering moment and it didn't happen overnight.

With the help of many people I trust who also have weathered severe martial storms, I woke up and took responsibility. I switched anger into empathy, ego into compassion, eye-rolling into acceptance, and asked Ryan to do the same, finding gratitude for all the years he allowed me my moment in the sun, now pausing to give him his own space to shine. It was his time. It was also time to forgive. I had felt abandoned by Ryan during most of my fertility struggles and needed to let that go. If I could just remind myself of the Ryan I met when he stepped into the Farmhouse doors, maybe the love song could end without me as the lonely romance novel reader, thirsty for more, and without Ryan as a boat with no water.

I was ready to ride shotgun, and relished that not only did I genuinely enjoy it, I began to cherish being his wife and felt great pride and respect for all we had built, endured and survived to get here. Who knows where this will take me? Maybe I'll even learn to cook more than Sunday sauce and party snacks, things like roasts and elaborate side dishes. Maybe it would resemble the life that Franklin longed for, and for that matter, one that maybe even Lucille dared to dream in her more vulnerable moments. Those romance novels piled high by her bed might have been cheesy or even a little racy, but I think what compelled her to read them was the same fantasy that everyone has—to be loved and seen for exactly who you are.

As the song reminds you, you can spend your life opening doors looking for—what? What if the door you've been looking for all along is the one that's the most familiar, the one to your own heart. And the person there is the one who's always been beside you and you're both ready to share each other's lead for what's next, and to write your own ending.

Tear for a Dear

"Picture a deer that's running from its predator, a wolf.... Once the deer gets away it starts to violently shake, and it's this shaking that releases all the chemicals and energy that was pent-up in both the freeze and flight responses. Due to this involuntary shaking, the deer may not experience trauma or stress related physical issues."

Amanda Gregory,
Trauma Psychotherapist

"Michael! Michael Lang! You look so good! You look so young!"

A very attractive woman in her early seventies was yelling at us while we stood on the stairs outside of The New York Historical Society. Inside the museum, the opening party celebrating Bill Graham and the Rock and Roll Revolution raged on, with an exhibit dedicated to "Exploring the life and work of the legendary music impresario who worked with the biggest names in rock music—including the Grateful Dead, Jefferson Airplane, Jimi Hendrix, Santana, Led Zeppelin, and the Rolling Stones." A huge portion of the exhibit was centered on my friend, the one who stood next to me on the stairs, Michael Lang and his iconic contribution to America music history, the Woodstock 1969 concert.

"Thanks May. Always good to see you." Michael responded in what I called his "humble mumble."

I stared in awe as May kissed him on both cheeks and walked away.

"Michael!" My mouth was literally hanging open. "Was that May Pang?"

Again, in his magical-pixie gentle tone, "Yes, yes it was. We used to hang. Ready to go?" he replied, entirely unphased by this encounter.

May Pang, for the uninitiated, worked for John Lennon and Yoko Ono as a personal assistant. But she was most famous for her and John's "lost weekend," a time in 1973 when

John and Yoko had separated, and with Yoko's encouragement, May became John's lover for a year and a half. It has been said that the song, "Woman" was written by John for Yoko as an apology for this "lost weekend" with May.

These were the type of things that would happen when I was with Michael.

I met Michael the year I turned twenty-nine. Ryan and I had just purchased our first home in Woodstock, New York, a modest two-bedroom, one bathroom farmhouse we called "Short Acre Farm," because it sat on just under an acre of land. Our tiny almost acre abutted a property that took up over 150 acres, so if you looked out our yard, you could see forever. The view was majestic. But who owned our view?

We had no idea.

The same year we bought the house, I had befriended a woman named Lee Blumer while planning a party for the Rolling Stones. While the Rolling Stones were an impressive client to add to my roster, Lee Blumer impressed me even more. This gentle hilarious, ex-hippie-turned-nightclub maven had a fantastic resumé which included working for Bill Graham, my beloved Monkees, the Woodstock concerts of 1969, 1994 and 1999, and ultimately became the woman to know in the New

York City nightclub scene, running the most exclusive venues of the 80s, 90s and now early 2000s. We bonded over the Rolling Stones extravaganza, with me stressing about keeping Keith Richards' Sunkist and Vodkas cold and the chicken satays warm, she with keeping the liquor authority and the Fire Marshall away as the party club was so new and hip, none of the proper permits necessary were actually in place. By the end of the party, I didn't want to be friends with Mick, I wanted to be best friends with Lee. Thirty years my senior, our unlikely but instant friendship was immediately sealed and would last until her death just days after her sixty-ninth birthday.

Lee was excited when I told her about our new Hudson Valley home as she said she spent a lot of time in that area and had loads of friends nearby. Lee had tons of friends everywhere, so I didn't pay much attention to this, but told her, "Sure! Call me the next time you're up. We have people over every weekend."

As both first-time homeowners and first-time catering company owners, these shindigs that Ryan and I hosted in our tiny country yard were some of the best parties of my career. "Ah, youth" I think now, as there is no way I would be as excited to host that many people, weekend after weekend, in that tiny house with one bathroom and no dishwasher. I still remember the hours I spent barefoot, basking in the afterglow of a party-gone-right and delighted to be hand washing what felt like hundreds of dishes and glasses after the last guest had either left or passed out on my lawn. I listened to soap stained records, as I would have to stop mid-rinse to turn them over. There was one mint green rotary phone I had purchased on eBay the day our offer was accepted, and it rang through the house like it was 1969. Since there was no wi-fi nor cell phone service, this was the only way for anyone to reach us. I loved that house.

Those days I was really into theme parties: midnight breakfasts, winter clambakes where I killed all the lobsters with bath water trying to keep them warm, a "find the dinner table" party, in which I greeted my guests with a flashlight and a flask and sent them on a hunt to find the perfectly set dinner I had spent hours creating in the field outside the perimeters of our property. One time, while waiting for the water delivery for our swimming pool, I dragged the dining room table to the deep end of the pool and hosted four friends for a candlelit dinner in this concrete cave. This tiny house, that we emptied our wedding savings to buy, had a 1950s shaped motel-style pool, complete with wave shaped rims and a footprint that was larger than the actual house. The water was always freezing because we were young and starting out and had no extra funds to turn on the heat—for that matter, it took us a year and half to realize the pool had no heater.

One weekend we were hosting our friend Pam, a big wig in the music business who was excited to spend some time with us upstate. We were shaking up a pitcher of martinis when the mint green phone rang. It was Lee. She too was upstate, staying at her friend's house for the weekend.

"Come on over. We're having martinis and, if we remember to make them, steaks. The more the merrier."

"Oh my God! Oh my God!" An hour later, I'll never forget the sound of Pam screaming while we were cutting potatoes on my vintage mint green kitchen island (it matched the phone).

When I looked out the window, I saw Lee and her friend walking up my driveway.

"You know Lee?" I asked Pam.

"No! That's Michael Lang?"

"Michael who?" I asked.

"Um. You just bought a house in Woodstock, and you don't know who Michael Lang is? The concert? 1969? Peace, love, and happiness? Janis Joplin? Jimi Hendrix? Brown acid? That's him!"

Michael Lang was in fact one of the four gentlemen responsible for pulling off THE MOST iconic concert in history, Woodstock 1969, the concert that defined a generation. And while there were three other partners in Woodstock Ventures producing the event, it was Michael's free spirit, his "cosmic pixie" type energy and his curly long hair and carefree-hippie attitude that made him the face of both the concert and his generation.

Delighted, of course, to have this Woodstock fixture over for dinner but now concerned he might be vegan, I welcomed Lee and Michael into our home, thrilled to find out that it was his majestic view and acreage behind our tiny plot. And he did in fact eat meat. What a trip!

It was just one of those magical Woodstock nights. We sat for hours talking, drinking, smoking, laughing. I was a goner: first Lee, now Michael, how would I ever be able to go back to hanging out with people my own age again? The stories they told were fascinating, using first names to describe cultural icons, like, "That time Janis and I were hanging out" as in Joplin! Or that time the Dalai Lama came to town and, "we just hung out and laughed." OR "It was the 60s Mary, everyone had herpes." But it was Michael's modest, magical, humble mumble that had me enchanted. The best way to describe that night was that Michael had arrived as a stranger and left as a part of our family.

And so our adventures together began.

Michael always called at the last minute to see if Ryan and I were free. Often, it was to "take a ride" and "check out something." I learned quickly that when that call came, you needed to drop everything, because you never knew what magical Michael day awaited you.

One time he rang me up and said, "I have to drop off some pictures; want to take a ride?" After a two-hour journey, we arrived on the set of the Ang Lee film *Taking Woodstock*, a dramatization of Michael's creation of the legendary Woodstock 1969 concert. It was his first visit to the set, so when he got out of the car, you could hear the proverbial record skip on its track, as all eyes were on him. I never felt cooler than that moment when I walked behind him, as he took in the magical recreations of his era: vintage motorcycles and cars, motels with retro neon signs, and a wardrobe department the size of an airplane hangar bursting with colorful hippie frocks. While Michael walked through his now recreated past, I could not stop watching people react to his presence, as though the messiah had arrived. The pictures he was dropping off were of the actual wooden concert stage that only he had, so the production designers could recreate it perfectly.

Other invites that came our way: "Do you want to have dinner with me and Arlo?" Guthrie, that is. "Wanna say hi to Stephen after his show?" Stills, of course. "I'm visiting with my friend Donovan, want to come?" Donovan just goes by Donovan. Opening night theater tickets, dinner at Sammy's Romanian, a drink at the Friar's Club. These were all casual invitations made available to us, like we were forever pals.

It was at this time of this new friendship that Ryan and I started to believe the magic of this man could rub off on us. If Michael could do what he did and define an entire generation with a dream, he flattered us to be kindred spirits. And just imagine the possibilities.

Michael's gentle teaching, without teaching, came at a time when I was striding into my thirties with my then-newish catering business, and thought I was onto something that could be IT. But he encouraged us to "go bigger." He never said this in so many words, but his mantra—to step into your truth and understand that no idea is too small—guided my entire decade. It was through Michael that I dreamed bigger, and worked harder.

He encouraged me to write and perform. He pointed out that my dinner parties were a type of theater. He realized that it was time for Ryan to fly and find a project that lit him on fire from within, something beyond our catering company, so he introduced Ryan to the parcel of land that would eventually become our hotel.

We were just starting out and he showed us the importance of believing in a dream but more importantly, he showed us humility and grace. Ryan loves to tell the story about a night he had dinner with Michael and how when they left the restaurant a fan was waiting outside to hand him guitar pics that he had printed to read "Thank you Michael." Ryan said the way he handled the interaction was so beautiful and humble and how after he kept a few pics for his own pocket, he handed a few to Ryan, like "here's some magic for you too." Michael did not hoard his light as some in his position would, he shared it. Lessons most people never get to witness by example from a friend who led a worldwide zeitgeist.

Years later, on the night the two of us left the Historical Society, we walked right past The Dakota, the famous building where John and Yoko lived and outside of which John was tragically murdered.

"You know what Michael? May is right. You are ageless, everyone says it. Forget about this music stuff," I was babbling, trying to distract him. Michael was overcoming another significant setback to the planning of the 2019 Woodstock 50th Anniversary and I was trying to cheer him up. It is virtually impossible to pull off something like Woodstock 1969 again, yet, Michael and Lee and a bunch of others who believed tried three more times! And while Woodstock '94 and '99 actually made it to the stage, not without controversy, the 50th planning phase was so brutal with egos and other producers involved, that it never actually came to fruition. Michael was now locked in legal issues and as always, the nail that sticks out the furthest always gets hit first so Michael was being torn apart in the media as "the face of Woodstock."

"You should have your own face cream line. Get on QVC. I can see it now: Tear of A Deer by Michael Lang!" The name sprung from my lips immediately as we had spent many days and nights in my Woodstock yard surrounded by beautiful deer. That Michael would be there to catch a baby deer's first tear made perfect brand sense.

He laughed. I loved making Michael laugh.

"Think Calvin Klein's *Obsession*. Lots of white smoke, camera pans back to a deer in the woods, dropping one solid tear, you are there to grab it, to place in an Elsa Peretti bottle and then you just whisper into the camera, "Tear of a Deer by Michael Lang.'"

That night would end up being the last night we would ever spend together in New York City. A month later Covid lockdown began and Michael was diagnosed with cancer. We were reduced to communicating via email or text as his illness and the fear of Covid kept us apart. After an almost two year battle he died and while it's always too soon for anyone who passes, it felt particularly too soon for this, my eternally youthful friend who still had so much to do.

Almost a year from his passing, while on a trip to Puerto Rico with my friend Grace, I confessed to her that I was struggling with releasing this new book out into the world. The fear of being attacked for sharing my truth loomed large, prompting me to confess to her that I might just "shelve this book" for later, perhaps in a kinder, more gentle time in history. I shared all of this with her as we made our way through a rainforest to swim in the Gozalandia Waterfalls, a walk and talk in which we both ended up releasing into the universe our various doubts and thoughts about "what comes next."

In typical Grace fashion, full of wisdom and random bits of knowledge, Grace paused and said, "Did you know that when a deer survives a near death experience, it begins to shake violently, releasing all the adrenaline and cortisol so that it does not experience trauma or stress related physical issues?"

I stood here in the center of that forest with a tear rolling down my face.

When you step out of your comfort zone and change the world, or if you have the capacity to dream without boundaries, you can become a moving target for those who cannot do the same. They will hurl their pain and insecurities at you. Michael was knocked down many times but like the deer, he shook it off and kept going. One last lesson for us.

Standing at that waterfall, I realized our silly little joke, "Tear of a Deer," my riff on Michael's imaginary face cream, should really be called "Tear for a Dear." Here's to my forever dear friend and all those he continues to inspire.

One of a Billion

It's perhaps not as bad as "Did I forget to mention the guest of honor is gluten-free?" but there's still another day-of-event call every caterer dreads.

"We're down a waiter."

"What? Why?"

"An audition. And supposedly the big one!"

While my booker (the person who books our waitstaff) on the other end of the line goes through every stage of grief and rage, I'm trying not to smile. Well no one can see me, so I do.

See, when I was eight years old, I dialed 411 and asked the operator for the number for NBC, my favorite network because it was home to my favorite show *Saturday Night Live*. When she gave me the number it felt like she knew she was bestowing it on me, a clearly very talented kid who was gifted with natural acting ability. Obviously this number was kept under wraps only to be shared with a select few. I instantly called the number, wowed by how many 4's were in the actual phone number for NBC Channel 4. When the switchboard operator answered, I threw my feet up onto my father's burl wood desk and with the cocky confidence of an eight-year-old with a Dorothy Hamill haircut that made her look exactly like Ralph Macchio I asked, "How do I get on TV?"

The operator laughed, "With hard work," and hung up.

The acting bug bit me hard and left its mark. My first stage was the elevated brick part of our living room fireplace. As my mother would say, "When Mary walks into a room she finds the most elevated part, and then makes it her stage." I loved doing impressions, making people laugh and writing and performing in my own one woman shows. Titles included: "I'm Running Away and It's All Your Fault," "Little Shabbos Goy (a Shabbos Goy can turn on lights, etc. for religious

Jews during the Sabbath—a job I weirdly and desperately wanted—and by the way, this was a musical***)," and "Out There It's 1985, In Here It's 1955," the latter taken straight from something my father often said when frustrated with my older sister wanting to do teenage things. On weekends, I would cast the neighborhood kids in my upcoming big, big movies, my dad even playing along and hired a proper director to record one of my films on a VHS recorder titled, *The Adventure Kids* (feel free to YouTube). My Papa Charlie was my best audience and biggest enabler. He would hoist me on top of the dining room table whenever company came over and encourage me to sing "The Sun Will Come Out Tomorrow." He also used to give me quarters to curse but that's a whole other story.

And still today when that potential life-changing break happens to one of my staff, I immediately think, "Wow, that's cool!" I imagine my waiter getting the role of lifetime that allows them to breeze into the

---

***Lyrics to Little Shabbos Goy
I'm your little Shabbos Goy
And I'm here to save the day
Make it easy on you
So that you can microwave

catering company the next morning and say, "Great knowing you all; I'm off to London to star in this new production of *Hamlet* on the East End." I've even been known to say to a member of my team I haven't seen for a while, "I'm happy you haven't been around. It means good things are happening for you—right?"

One of the greatest joys of my career, and one of the reasons I keep the lights on, is that for the last twenty years, MGCE, my catering company, has served as a virtual Ellis Island for creatives: actors, writers, dancers, and musicians who arrive in New York with big dreams and empty pockets. They remind me of myself when I landed here in 1997, chasing that same dream that once prompted me to cold call the NBC switchboard. I was going to make it on Broadway or get on *The Guiding Light*—both equally impressive to me. But the closest I ever got to this dream was work as an extra.

Extra work, when you are in your twenties and think you are going to be the next Meryl Streep, can be the most humiliating, soul-crushing work one can take. You are often told of your "extra" booking the night before or sometimes on the same day and must drop everything you are doing to arrive on set where you very quickly realize there are principal actors and there are extras and these two worlds very rarely, if ever collide. You are put in your place immediately. Principals get their own trailers, where they are waited on hand-and-foot and fed anything they desire. Extras are demanded to gather, cattle-like, in sexy places like church basements or defunct public school gymnasiums, and given no real instruction except to wait. Extras are fed what appear to be the leftovers from the discarded principal actors' meals: half sheet trays of picked over stuffed shells and white mush that resembles chicken. One time, a salad I was eating had one rogue dried cranberry and one tiny almond, alerting me to slightly unhygienic fact that my salad had been picked over earlier by a star sitting in her heated trailer, her salad heaping with cranberries and almonds, while I froze my ass off sitting on a kindergartner's desk in a vacant building.

When they do finally call you "to set," you once again very quickly realize that you will not be hanging with Tom Hanks, and that if they could replace you with a wicker chair, they would be more than happy to do just that.

I took tons of these extra jobs, hoping each time, someone in power would see that special something in me, grab me from the extras line up, give me a part, and a salad loaded with deluxe dried fruit and nuts. I danced for hours (to no music) in an empty warehouse in Jersey City for a whole week for Whit Stillman's *The Last Days of Disco*, only to end up on the cutting room floor. I dressed like a street walker in high heels and a skirt that was so small it could've been mistaken for a cocktail napkin, shivering on a street in Queens for days for the made-for-TV movie about Sammy "The Bull" Gravano. The moment the director said "cut!" I took my position in the same spot from which I was to walk back and forth, back and forth, back and forth, during the shoot on that wintry day, while two assistants would run out covering the principal actress literally inches away from me in a fur blanket while she awaited the camera to roll again. They even swapped out her heels for warm boots while she sipped from a mug of steaming hot tea. Again, this week of work never yielded me any actual screen time. It was hard, brutal even, and, most notably, not any fun. Wasn't this supposed to be fun?

The rejection, the waiting, the non-glamour torture of being so close yet so far, or as the Howard Jones' power ballad says, just a toe in the water, you're not allowed to swim. It all took its toll on me and one day I simply gave up.

I didn't have "it." I was going to have to live with that.

But I'd be lying if I said that itch ever went away, so one of the ways I manage to scratch it is watching the hundreds of waiters that we employ actually stick it out. My new not-so-secret guilty pleasure was hearing about their audition or screen time successes, and, often, to the detriment of my own company's success, I would hold back a waiter in the service line, a plate of hot food in their hand that is meant to be served to an A-Lister, just to hear the end of their "I had four lines!" victory lap. Their joy was my joy. So while I continued to work hard, like the NBC operator advised me, I was putting in my time, not on screen but behind a caterer's tray. Until one day, fantasy became reality, I got my own Big Break.

The Showtime hit *Billions* created by the amazing Brian Koppleman had become famous for giving New York City foodies a chance in the spotlight. Real culinary stars like David Chang, Daniel Boulud and Missy Robbins playing themselves with perfectly placed cameos. Never in a million (ha, billion) years would I put myself in the same category of these culinary icons, but lo and behold, Brian got a copy of my book *Tiny Hot Dogs* and must have read the "If You Can't Join 'Em, Serve 'Em" part and thought, "Hmmm, we need a high-end caterer for a party scene. Let's give this little wannabe Jewish girl/aspiring actress a shot and cast her." In my world, we call this a mitzvah and I will forever be grateful to Brian for giving me the chance to live out my dream on screen.

A cameo on *Billions*, a part written for me, to be played by me. I had arrived so far in the catering world that I was being asked to play myself on one of the hottest shows on TV. I know that when that call came in, the proper response should have been, "What a great plug for my catering company!" Instead, I was deep in my own internal dialogue, thinking, "Is this it? Has my time finally come?

The wild part of my big break was that it was scheduled during the early rumblings of Covid. The days leading up to the shoot, I prayed and prayed, "Dear Lord, please don't let them shut down before they film my scene." And in fact, we shot literally the day before the entire New York City entertainment industry was closed. Prayers answered.

When I was asked if I wanted to pick the extras in my scene, I gladly pulled in my business partner Michele and chef Michael—an absolute no-brainer decision because without them, there would be no MGCE. On the day of the shoot I nearly cried happy tears when I was taken to my very own trailer, and a knock on the door was an assistant asking what I wanted for lunch. Yes, you guessed it. I ordered a salad with cranberries and almonds and joyfully ate the whole thing while hair and makeup prepared me for my scene. I sort of envied Michele and Michael for seeing this opportunity for exactly what it was: a fun day on a TV set. A story to share with friends and family. Nothing more. Nothing less. But for me? I was deep in my head, thinking about what I was sure was going to be a complete change in life career pivot following this appearance. Surely this was going to be my moment to shine and to be discovered for the great talent that I had always been. I mean, clearly these fine television folks would see past me as "the caterer" and write me into the show as a principal, right?

As I waited for the party scene to start, I remembered my earlier experiences as an extra. I felt now more relaxed, armed with the wisdom, maturity, and patience of someone who understands the value of a hard day's work. How well I had learned the true dedication it takes to make it happen whatever year it is. If I could go back I would no longer be so insulted by the picked-over cuisine and the grubby holding pens. I would join forces with my new quirky friends doing exactly what I was doing, ruminating in the excitement of their dreams, the same way I cheer on my waiters today.

Maybe I gave up too soon, not because I didn't want it but because I wasn't ready to jump through all the hoops to make it happen. I did jump, but through a different set of hoops. In the twenty years since my last work as an extra, I've burned as many heels tap-tapping across marble floors at galas as I would have pacing the sidewalks, mimicking a hooker. I almost turned my hands perma-red from peeling beets for an Oscar party when my chef was felled by the flu. Maybe I wasn't committed back in the day, but, oh boy, did I know what commitment felt like now!

I decided right then and there to reactivate my profile on Backstage, upload new headshots, check the casting notices obsessively, all just to land that "Deli Patron" blur in the background on the *Marvelous Mrs. Maisel* or "Upscale Party Guest" backside shot on *Succession*. I mean, who better to play the backside of an upscale party guest than me?

So you never know. I may be part of a conga line with a pineapple on my head or a passenger on an airplane about to go down. Meet the new middle-aged version of the girl still waiting for *Saturday Night Live* to answer the phone.

Tantric Makeover

A few months before Gala was born, a close friend told me that I should start having lots of sex with Ryan because, "once the baby comes you won't have sex for years."

Years?

Already, Ryan and I had not had sex in what felt like years leading up to Gala's arrival, due to a combination of fertility drug madness, multiple miscarriages and the debilitating pain I suffered from endometriosis. Combine all of that with the almost eighteen years of monogamous sex we had shared, we were, to paraphrase Liz Tuccillo's best-selling book, "just not that into each other."

Still, I could not escape the horror that this

little piece of friendly sexual advice brought on. Was I never going to have sex with Ryan again? I needed help, or rather, we needed help. I started to look up sex therapists, swingers' retreats, sexual surrogates (AKA hookers), and decided that one week at a tantric sex seminar titled *Intimacy and The Sexual Experience,* led by Dr. Elsbeth Meuth and Freddy Zental Weaver, tucked away at an ashram in the Berkshires, was just what we needed.

"Like, we're going to have sex with other people kind of place?" Ryan asked as I dropped the news one day prior to informing him to pack seven days worth of sweatpants; the packing sheet instructed us to bring "easily removable clothing."

"I have no idea," was my honest response.

As you may have guessed already, I'm not a huge researcher or an over-thinker of any variety. My tombstone will mostly read: "Not practical in the least, here lies Mary. She never really knew what would happen one day to the next and she leaves us with an inbox filled with 78,039 unread emails."

I started my businesses on impulse. I applied to only one school for my daughter and decided to let it ride and not submit paperwork to another dozen or so other programs, like most of the over-scheduled, over-zealous

New Yorkers I know and love. I decided to move us out of and back to NYC on whims on more than one occasion. I planned most of our family's long distance travel at the last minute because I get restless and suddenly read something that inspires me to pick up and go. Once there, nine times out of ten, I changed our return dates, extend our trip or decided to squeeze in a visit to another nearby spot.

I had actually visited Kripalu, where our Berkshires sex retreat was taking place, two other times for different kinds of health resets and had also booked both trips last minute. I did not obsess over what would be in store for me once I arrived. This works well for me. For Ryan, not so much.

Ryan prefers plans, maps and directions. He travels better with planned snacks for the car and carefully packed bags with practical solutions in case we run out of gas or get delayed in arriving at our destination. To this day, he cannot believe that I successfully mothered baby Gala without carrying around one of those two hundred pound diaper bags that other mothers schlepped with them everywhere. Ryan needs to know what's next, what's coming, who's coming. So, in this case, not only did I tell him that I was unsure of with whom we were having sex, but added cheekily, that if we were lucky, everyone would be "coming." Instantly he was happily packing.

This was Ryan's first retreat of any kind, so it took him a few days getting used to the share circles, and the organic, white flour-free, sugar-free, and booze-free diet they were serving up in the high school style cafeteria, which in turn made us very gassy. So in between learning how to "heal" my yoni (vagina) and his lingham (penis), we were farting up a storm. How's that for sexy?

A visual I feel is important to share is that leading the twenty couples in our "share" circle was Elsbeth and her lover (her term) Freddy. Elsbeth is a five foot tall German woman with a thick accent that commands respect and Freddy is a 6'7" black man who draws out words like "yeeeeessssss" and "pleeeeeeasssure." They wore beach attire to each session, lots of sarongs, to allow their "base chakras" to stay light and free.

So, did we all have sex with each other? Did we watch Elsbeth and Freddy have sex? Not even close. Surprisingly, and with more than a little relief, we found the workshop to be a very hygienic, respectful, caring, supportive environment that was not really about sex. It was about compassion, healing sexual trauma, putting your partner first, learning how to receive and how to give and how to break the habit of only being good at either receiving or giving. I won't share any of Ryan's intimate findings but guess who needed to work on receiving more?

After eighteen years together, we were surprised to learn things we never knew about each other. The "sex" parts were assignments given to us to practice at night in the privacy of our cramped ashram rooms. Each night we would take turns inviting the other for a "healing session," and something I'll reveal about those assignments is that Sting looks amazing for a reason!

The retreat worked for us and the majority of the other couples. One couple sadly broke up mid-week when one of them arrived at the "share" circle alone and confessed that he simply could not heal her yoni so she had packed up and headed back to the city. After a week with Elsbeth, Freddy and the strangers, Ryan and I had reconnected, revisited the reason we first fell in love and had more orgasms than we'd had in our collective lifetimes. Even the farting stopped. The retreat glow was shining bright in both of us, and we committed to this new way of life together.

On the last day, we stopped by the gift

shop, like one does after spending a week at an ashram, inspired to continue our life change via retail therapy. We purchased meditation pillows, sarongs, *Kama Sutra* oils, Mala beads, and even yoni eggs. For the uninitiated, a yoni egg is a jade egg that a woman places into her vagina to strengthen her pelvic floor, which, upon our return home, became an ongoing joke. At the dinner table I would drop a dinner fork and apologize, saying, "Oops, my yoni egg fell out again."

Determined not to turn everything into a joke, I took things a step further and while finishing the conversion of our guest bedroom into a nursery, I turned my small writing cottage into a *Kama Sutra* den for us to use, prior and post Gala's arrival. This would be our secret lovers spot, encouraging us to invite each other in for "sessions" which we did a few times until the baby arrived.

Then, poof!

Just like my friend had warned me, the massage oils dried up, the yoni egg turned into an ornamental paperweight that sat on top of my desk and it would be years before we would invite each other to another "yoni" or "lingham" healing session.

But every once in awhile, he'll ask me how my "yoni" is doing and I'll respond with

a question about the state of his "lingham,"
reminding us that while my pal was correct,
it is possible to say "Yeeeeeeessssssss." Just like
riding a bicycle.

Love, Mary

For years I followed food priestess Ruth Reichl's tweets:

"Pale sky. New mown grass. Tart, icy lemonade. Subtle salad: thinly sliced duck breast, apricots, arugula, shards of parmesan, balsamic."

"Caviar. Blini. Habanero salsa, shock waves of fire, electrical sparks. Soothing softness of polenta and mascarpone."

And for years, I fantasized that if I would just step out of my hectic New York City life, give up the stress, the chaos, the constant movement of the city, and surrender to a calm, peaceful life in the country, I too would look out my window each morning serenely amazed at the dewy field, all the while a fluffy pat of artisan-churned butter melted onto my freshly baked blueberry muffin.

Bliss, right?

The pandemic gave me and a lot of other city dwellers the chance to try this on and believe me when I tell you that my country-morning tweets (if I tweeted, which I don't), would have read a bit more like this:

"Gagootz (what we Italians call zucchini) dead in my failure-of-a-garden, pizza from the night before heating in the toaster oven sans foil to catch the burnt cheese drippings. How joyful the chime of the clock when it strikes noon, ice filling my shaker. Vodka is nice any time of day."

Yeah, I didn't take to the country in the same way Ruth Reichl did.

Obviously this is not the part when I tell you how hard I tried to reinvent myself in the mold of Ruth, Pioneer Woman or anyone else who rules in the drag of rural domestic bliss. I did not double down on growing and harvesting lavender for bath salts, didn't grind my own cornmeal for my Thanksgiving stuffing, and I certainly didn't make quilts out of my old concert tees for that ironic "rock and roll chick learns to craft" vibe.

What I quickly realized was that if I was

ever going to learn to love living in the country, I'd have to shake things up, and not just the vodka and ice I was prepping for cocktail hour.

One of my favorite movies is the 1980s Diane Keaton classic *Baby Boom*. I'd presume anyone reading me by now would have also seen this movie over a hundred times, but in case one of you haven't, quick recap: Diane Keaton plays a powerful New York City executive who happens to "inherit" a baby from a distant relative. In the time it takes for her to try to find a proper adoptive home, she bonds with the baby and her company gives her the boot for daring to take the hour or two to manage a family. So she gives it all up for a gorgeous country spread in Vermont that presents endless broken down house problems until she finally starts jarring homemade baby food during her winter isolation and frustration, and ultimately makes a killing in the new trendy organic baby food market. Oh, she also lands a hot veterinarian along the way.

My Diane Keaton redux was gonna to be a breeze as I didn't need the hot vet and had a solid house. I was going to start a frozen food company in the Hudson Valley, party boxes of luxe *hors d'oeuvres* that were based on my catering company's "greatest hits." They would be called *Love, Mary* as they were indeed an edible love note to you, my sweet customers. This idea checked every box. I would be engaging with and employing locals with whom I was hoping to establish a deeper connection. I would have a new base of operations just miles away from my mountainside home, and my husband Ryan's hotel, allowing me to drop Gala at her country day school and zip off to work amid blue skies and sunshine. And I'd have a purpose, which was most certainly needed. Left to my own devices, I was coming to the realization that I was no Ruth Reichl-in-training. I had gotten way too comfortable with mid-day cocktails, as if my guardian angel was a 1950s chain-smoking housewife, flicking ashes on my head while granting me permission to behave badly.

I had already started one successful company, Mary Giuliani Catering & Events, which entered its fifteenth year during the pandemic, and I had done that with very limited funds. How hard could this be?

Just as Keaton in *Baby Boom* sat up late nights studying baby food chains, I dove headfirst into all things appetizer frozen food: Packaging, dry ice, logos, stickers, tiny food molds. Thankfully, I found an incredibly talented husband and wife team, Luc and Pika, who achieved local and national success by preparing and distributing their home-cooked sundries all over the country, and all based in their very impressive Kingston, NY warehouse and prep kitchen just a fifteen minute drive away.

Luc was a magician and delightfully played along with my dream while I blurted out my wish list for this inaugural collection, pastrami on rye tartlets, lasagna Bolognese bites, everything pigs in a pie, beet clouds, chicken pot pies and mac and cheese cupcakes. The *Love, Mary* collection was on its way. I envisioned Whole Foods samplings, me clad in oven mitts and apron, popping treats into Oprah's mouth on air—you know me, the works.

While Luc was managing the calculations and ratios needed to take our Mary Giuliani Catering's signature bites and recreating them into recipes that would be made with affordable ingredients which froze well and wouldn't bust the budget, I was working around the clock on marketing plans, FDA regulations, ingredient labels and of course, beautiful packaging. My first big idea had the food packaged on individual trays that popped out of a box that looked exactly like an Easy Bake Oven kind of package. Then, I got the price for these magical trays and prototype boxes and realized that no one (other than the Sultan of Brunei) would be able to afford my fantasy party box. Thankfully, Luc and Pika presented me with a much cheaper and realistic option, so the *Love, Mary* collection would still go from freezer to oven but not with such an extreme sticker shock price tag.

I was determined our product would arrive during the first Covid holiday season, so customers who were sick of cooking for their families and friends, could simply pop a few of my little nibbles in the oven, pour themselves a drink and poof—party! But because of my self-imposed deadline, I rushed everything. Anyone who told me to wait a beat until the idea could be further flushed out, or, worse said to wait another year until I worked out a proper business plan, were quickly sidelined from the team.

I spent my first full time Hudson Valley winter in an unheated warehouse wearing gloves of wool for warmth and latex for food safety, as well as hat and thermal underwear. I assembled cardboard boxes, applied *Love, Mary* stickers to each tray, and filled mini vials of seasoning salts that would accompany my tiny treats which were indeed actually made with absolute love. Sometimes a few extra hands would come in and help me, but mostly I was alone. While hand-building my dream, I listened to inspiring entrepreneurial podcasts, and a playlist that included both Carly's Simon's hits from *Baby Boom* and *Working Girl*, as well as "Eye of the Tiger" and "Don't Stop Me Now," again on repeat.

On snow days from school, or, when I felt like letting us both sleep in, I brought Gala to the warehouse with me and we worked side by side, stickering boxes, mixing up seasoning salts, yakking with the staff, marveling at the enormous vats in the kitchen and storage in freezers. Talk about a Willy Wonka moment for both of us! There is no greater career satisfaction than taking a dream and showing it off to your own daughter. Supportive pals stopped by the warehouse and were promptly ordered to wash their hands, glove up and get to work. Over those months, I think my hands touched almost every box of our initial eight hundred box run. I even kissed some boxes (sorry Covid!) before the UPS delivery folks arrived to pick up orders. Every time my writing partner Abbe stopped by, we broke into the theme song from *Laverne & Shirley*, dancing around the cold kitchen in gloves and hairnets.

Love, Mary was picked up by Macy's and Bloomingdales. I didn't get to hand-feed

Oprah but the collection was featured in *O Magazine*'s Valentine's favorites list.

I was clearly on a roll. I boogied around the warehouse to "Ain't No Stoppin' Us Now" and got into discussions with a few different companies who wanted to co-brand with us and present other frozen food collections. However, they kept pointing out that the pricing on the collection was still too high, but I presumed this was a minor thing. We were launched.

One day, while contemplating investing in another run of boxes, I decided it might be time to ask the advice of one of my most brutally honest friends who also had a great head for business.

"Do you think it's a bad sign that I've had zero repeat customers?"

"What do you mean, zero?"

"People order one box but never a second one. The feedback is that they like the food, but the box is just too expensive. I know, I know. I should have taken my time and done a cost analysis." Look at me, using words like cost analysis.

"Bad sign," said my friend without hesitation. "Close it up immediately. Or, simplify and then ask yourself, do you even want to be in the retail food business?"

He was right. I did not. I loved it. But the infrastructure wasn't there, and I was having a hard time finding others who wanted to freeze their butts off in the warehouse for another season while we waited to see if we would turn a profit. It was a labor of love, hell, I called the collection *Love, Mary* for a reason, but it was my labor of love and no one else was feeling as romantic as me. Especially anyone with a working calculator.

So, Ruth Reichl, you made me think I could do anything in that fresh mountain air. And Ruth, you were right. I could possibly do anything. I built up another business from scratch, but unlike the first one I birthed, this one, no matter how much I loved it, couldn't make anyone any money. I felt there was no "where there's a will, there's a way" message calling out to me in the early spring at my house as I watched the light brighten over the Catskill Mountains and I prepped some drinks for friends with a few extra boxes of *Love, Mary* apps heating up in the toaster oven.

So, it seemed like my *Baby Boom* moment was over. But I still love that pivotal scene in the movie where Diane Keaton has left her fabulous Manhattan career and life and moved to the house in the country that keeps breaking down. She discovers she has no water and when the contractor explains to her the need to replace the well to her house and the cost associated with it, she exclaims: "I just want to turn on the faucet and have water. I don't want to know where it's coming from!"

She's right. Through my frozen food fantasy, I learned some valuable lessons about the back end of business. But I'm also right. A labor of love is worth seeing through completion. And in both instances, sometimes you just want to turn the faucet on and off, and move on.

Frozen Pelvis

"You have one of the worst cases of endometriosis I've ever seen. Stage Five, for sure." A doctor with the the most horrific bedside manner, surely taken from a page out of Nurse Ratchet's handbook, states with no sense of softness in his tone or his hand, his fingers poking around inside of me as if he were prepping a chicken for the oven. "If I were you, I would walk over to the hospital ER and admit yourself for emergency surgery and ask for me to do it. It will take me 10-12 hours to undo this mess." Sidebar: any doctor that calls your reproductive system a mess should have their medical license revoked.

Numbed by the fact that there was a Stage 5 ANYTHING happening inside my body, and now completely shaken by his rude and ice cold demeanor, I needed to find another doctor quickly. This was NOT my guy. I quickly moved into emergency WebMD LIVE mode, when you scroll and a possible diagnosis scares you so much that you scroll again so you can settle on the one that gives you some relief— the one that ends with "or it could just be gas." I Googled a new doctor from the waiting room of Dr. Hideous (Endosisters DM me: I'll tell you his name. He's in New York City and boasts LOTS of celebrity clients, as if their uteruses are more special than ours) and thankfully, I found one that would take my begging pleas for an appointment "TODAY, as in RIGHT NOW PLEASE!"

As I walked down the street, to now visit the 12th doctor I was about to see since the onset of my reproductive trauma, tears streamed down my face. I realized I was at the "But, wait there's more?" portion of my battle with this largely misunderstood and terribly undiagnosed beast of a reproductive (and now full organ onslaught) disease. Starting with my first period when I passed out from the pain in my bathroom floor, causing my then 12-year-old best friend to run and get my mother because "this doesn't seem normal," to years of both physical and mental pain, which resulted in me almost losing my mind and most certainly, losing my fertility. My lifestyle (stress on top of stress) and the methods I used to numb the constant chronic pain was a recipe for disaster, and there were times leading up to the birth of my daughter Gala (born via an incredible saint of a surrogate) when I was ready to give up on EVERYTHING. Once Gala arrived, a lot of the mental pain went away with each smile or laugh, snuggle, or coo she threw my way. Slowly, the pieces of kiddie art I longed to hang on my refrigerator started clearing away the blues; the macaroni necklace that I wore more until it disintegrated around my neck was better than Bulgari, and that first, "I love you Mom," made all those years of pain, longing, desperation, anger, and fear feel like the very least I had to endure for this miracle of a child.

But this disease no matter how much I tried to ignore it or numb it with my determination to be "normal" never let up for a minute. One doctor described my chronic pain once with this comparison, "it's like you've held your hand on a hot oven for over twenty years, never removing it once. Your nervous system is shot. How you even function on a daily basis is kind of a miracle. You do what for a living!? Are you kidding me? How is it that you're even standing up?"

Thank God, the moment I arrived at Dr. Masa Kanayama's office, I knew I was in the right place. He gently performed the exact same procedures of The Asshole Doctor on 5th Avenue, but with great care, and by asking permission before he did anything during my exam that he knew caused a lot of "normal" women discomfort and that was excruciating for women suffering from endo. It was the first exam in twenty years that I felt like a doctor understood me, and this beast of a disease. While he confirmed that yes, my case would indeed be difficult, it was nothing he could not tackle and felt confident that he would give me some form of relief. A chance at a pain-free life. After the exam, I met him in his office and tears continued to stream down my face as he took thoughtfully took time to explain everything to me, even offering scientific hypothesis that since my ancestors were from Sicily, a volcanic area, that this could had led to my disease as there is a high number of endo-patients are from Volcanic regions. Made sense, as if anyone asked me to describe my pelvic region with just one word, it would certainly be Volcano.

And then he dropped this on me, "You have a frozen pelvis."

Straight to WebMD, I go as he's writing up the script for my surgery.

Frozen pelvis happens when these adhesions "glue" pelvic organs together or wrap around organs. The adhesions can also:

- Attach to the lining of the abdomen or pelvic walls
- Create web-like structures between organs
- Extend to deeper tissues and affect the nerves, lymph nodes, and muscle layers of organs

As the adhesions grow deeper, they cause soft tissues and organs in the pelvis to harden and become rock-like. Other terms for frozen pelvis include "end-stage endometriosis" or "terminal endometriosis."

Hey, can't say I don't do things to the extreme.

As I was being prepped for a six-hour surgery to "unfreeze" my frozen pelvis, I was terrified, as you can imagine. I had spent the weeks leading up to this very surgery that I had put off for years, thinking everything was my last go-round, the treasured and the trivial alike. It was my last trip to Montauk, my last trip to Hillstone for my beloved spinach artichoke dip (truly, just order it), my last time getting eyelash extensions, my last haircut, where I tearfully hugged my stylist saying, "if I don't make it, at least I won't be gray."

And don't even get me started about everything I did with Gala during those "last" few weeks...

"Mom, why are we going to FAO Schwarz again?" asks no seven year old ever but, in all fairness, this was our third trip in a week.

We went to what felt like every museum in Manhattan, all my favorite restaurants, my favorite store (Fishs Eddy by the way), and on our walks to school I even started to impart wisdom on her that really should've stayed shelved until she was older. Things like "One day Gala, you will fall in love, and I don't care if it's with a man or a woman or a woman who wants to be a man, or a man who was once a woman who now wants to be a man again, as long as your love is true. That's all that matters."

"Men want to be women?"

My effort to reduce incredibly complex grown-up ideas into bite-sized pieces of child-appropriate "love is good, so love" language would be better coming from public television specials.

So, I sat down and wrote Gala a tear soaked

"I love you, goodbye, thank you for being you" letter, in case this was indeed The End.

Dear Gala,

If you remember nothing else from this letter, here are my final takeaways for you . . . .

Bachelorette Party Etiquette

Try to avoid them at all costs, but if you have to attend, here are two rules. Never wear a hat on your head shaped like a penis and never give the affirmative when someone asks you, "Are you gals here for a bachelorette party." Instead, do like Mama did and respond, almost offended. "NO! We were all dancers from the Broadway hit *Cats* and this is our reunion weekend." Then teach all your gals to hold their hands up, make paw-like movements and hiss.

Never Say Things On Saturday Night That You Do Not Mean On Sunday Morning

Your mother once woke up to an entire band that she met at The Memory Motel in Montauk (yes, the one that The Rolling Stones made famous) on Saturday night ringing your grandparent's doorbell on Sunday morning. As I hid in the bathroom, your grandmother informed the group of heavily tattooed, hungover men who claimed they were invited by Mary for brunch or Sunday Sauce, or possibly both, that "My daughter says things on Saturday that she does not mean on Sundays" after which, not waiting for any response from the band, she closed the door, pulled me out of the bathroom and gave me The Look.

Yentl, NEVER A Bad Idea

No matter where you are or what you are doing, if your TV lands on an airing of *Yentl*, stop and watch it until the end. The earlier in life your appreciation for Mandy Patinkin begins, the richer it shall be.

Have Your Own Dance Or Your Own Song

Almost two decades ago, I perfected a routine to the Britney Spears hit, "Hit Me Baby One More Time" that I began to perform at any event that had a dance floor. Weddings, bar/bat mitzvahs, reunions. It slays every time. Even in my mid/late forties, I'm still slapping the ground and shaking my hips. Pick a song, choreograph it and own it! Or, be like your grandfather, who co-opted the song "Please Don't Talk About Me When I'm Gone" that he sings at every occasion. It's only awkward when he sings it at funerals.

Speaking of dancing . . .

Dance with your Top Off at a Gay Bar, at Least Once

Your mother is proud to say that she was one of very few women to attend the closing night of The Roxy, one of the most famous dance clubs in New York City. When I got to the coat check and saw all the handsome gents checking their shirts, I made the decision that I too should do the same. Obvious tip: gay men provide extremely safe female spaces.

Wear Your Monkees Freak with Pride

When you were three years old, I took you to the Lincoln Center Tree Lighting where Micky Dolenz was performing. We sat in the front row and at the precise moment Mickey sang "I'm a believer!" he pointed directly at you! This day was as important to me as your baptism. There's a responsibility that comes with defending one of the greatest bands of all time. Fight for the freak in you and all the freaks out there always. Also thank your father for fighting me on naming you Micky Dolenz Giuliani.

Befriend Your Elders

And by elders, I mean at least thirty years your senior. Some of the most amazing and inspiring friendships I've had have been with people older than me. They care way less about what others think, understand more about life from a zen-like "this too shall pass" attitude and can even get away with a little non-PC humor, for which I'm more than a little envious. Elders often do all the things I've told you are bad for you, they'll drink, smoke, say naughty words, even fart at the dinner table, all unapologetically. If we're lucky, you'll be old like them someday too.

Live In New York City A While

There is truly no greater place in the world in which you can grow, dream, eat hot dogs and fall in love. New York will keep you young and alive. If you are open to it, you can literally fall in love with something new every single day of your life there. Yes, we are all just tiny specks of sand in a sea of billions and billions of other specks. Sometimes you are shining brightly under cloudless skies, ablaze in your glory. Sometimes, you are in the deepest trenches of the ocean, buried under the weight of a trillion gallons of dark swirling water. Every twelve hours you can go to sleep and start afresh the next day. Step outside and turn a different corner to discover a whole new world. You might just inch a little closer to the surface, but if you've momentarily reached the beach, lay back and dry off in the warm sun.

Do Things (Or Don't Do Things), For Real, Not Just For Social Media

Since I'm past my selfie-in-bikini prime and simply cannot bring myself to photograph another piece of food, I chose to make my social media identity, "Look at me I'm writing." I made this horrible mistake repeatedly for the last two years, creating elaborate environments in which I'd soon be writing, just so I could snap a photo and post it on social media, essentially saying this but not necessarily doing this. While I very much enjoyed traveling to romantic, idyllic writing haunts, including, but not limited to, a cottage near Snedens Landing, a desk with an oceanfront view, and a stone house with a fireplace in the Adirondacks, the posts didn't exactly live up to the hype. Once I hash-tagged books, I spent the rest of my "writing time" doom-scrolling on my phone, rewatching full seasons of *That Girl* and *The Sopranos* and taking naps. How many books could have been written if I was writing as much as I was posting about how I was writing?

And finally, please promise me you will find doctors, friends and family that believe your pain if you are ever suffering. That hear you when you say, "this doesn't feel right" and fight like hell until they do. If your mama would have found her voice sooner, learned how to share louder and didn't grow up during a time when Melissa Manchester's "Don't Cry Out Loud" was the number one song in America, then my great defrost both physical and mental . . . may have never needed to happen.

How to Lose Friends and Influence No One

I had breakfast with Steve Martin and said not one word because I was afraid it was all true—that he was not *The Jerk* but A Jerk! Okay, having breakfast with him is not entirely true. I was invited to breakfast by one of my favorite New Yorkers, my mentor, and the anointed King of Retail. A notoriously private person who would no doubt prefer to remain nameless, so for thisone, I task you to "think big."

While waiting in a diner on the Upper East Side picked out by this oracle, I reminisced how we had met, how many kind and selfless acts I saw him complete not just for me but for countless others. I considered what a talisman he's been for me. A good luck charm as well as sometimes the bearer of not-so-great news or opinions because he knows he is counted upon for support as well as reality checks for those who love him.

I was relishing what was sure to be a much overdue catch up between us when I realized that the only other person in the diner was a gray haired man sitting in the booth facing directly in front of me was Steve Martin. Yes, my Steve Martin. My Navin Johnson—*The Jerk* himself.

My alter ego, my inspiration, my entire reason for being, well, me! We made eye contact before I hastily pretended to be looking at the door, anticipating my breakfast date's arrival, and he went back to his coffee. That was it.

In case you didn't read my last book, *Tiny Hot Dogs* (available at finer bookstores and in copious stacks in my parent's basement), I recounted how from a young age I chose to be a delusional optimist just like Navin Johnson, Martin's character in the Carl Reiner classic film. I chose to see opportunity in disappointment; to believe that anything was possible; to believe that even the smallest things could become BIG. The same way Navin Johnson saw his name in the phone book for the first time and believed it would lead him to fame and fortune. The same way Navin Johnson believed that working as a gas station attendant could lead him to becoming the next president of Texaco Oil. At eight years old this became my M.O., my *modus operandi*, all because my father had brought home a VHS tape player and that one fateful movie.

Now here I was, waiting for one of New York's most beloved CEOs and literally face to face with the man who brought to life the fictional character that I had spent more than half my life emulating—let's call it what it was: worshiping. I needed quick advice as I would have only one chance to make a first impression, any impression.

First text: to my favorite dream collaborator Abbe who immediately text-screams in delight, then points out that this will no doubt make a great story. Her next idea is for me to pick up his check; that this would be a boss move and a natural intro.

Next text: to my best friend Annie, who was the only witness to my lunch with Robert DeNiro almost twenty years ago. Annie, then nine months pregnant, left her uptown confines to hide behind a menu in the downtown restaurant where I dined with "Bob" because after a chance meeting at an *SNL* after-party he asked to meet me for coffee (it's a great story that is also featured in my last book *Tiny Hot Dogs* that, did I mention is available where all books are sold) and I needed her to back up my story that would obviously be told over and over.

Annie also understood the true significance of this sighting and offered to sneak out of her Pilates class, run home to grab a copy of *Tiny Hot Dogs* and run it to the diner in time for me to sign it to him. I immediately called her off as even I knew that would be way too much.

Final text: to my mentor, begging him to get to the diner as fast as possible as I'm confident he and Steve move in the same circles. In my mind, he will walk in, and introduce me to Steve and Bingo! We'd all become fast pals.

But time was NOT on my side.

By now Steve is halfway through his poached eggs and toast (he likes a lot of fresh ground pepper, by the way), as I sweat and scheme, pretending not to be wholly freaking out by the near miracle of this sighting. No less the question of whether I should try to do anything about it.

I did absolutely nothing.

Moments after Steve paid his check and left, my breakfast pal slid into my booth opposite me.

"Do you know Steve Martin?" Was the first question that flew from my mouth.

" Yeah. A little bit. So what did you decide to do about . . . ." He was off and running, asking me questions about a business idea I was pondering. Steve Martin was already forgotten in his mind, just another guy having breakfast in a diner.

After receiving advice on a few business issues, we kibbitzed about friends, family and the general state of the world. While saying our goodbyes, I was tempted to ask a few more questions about Steve Martin. Extremely important questions like, "How well do you know him?" or maybe, "How well will I know him after you introduce us, or when fate brings us together for diner eggs again?" and then I remembered exactly why I chose to do nothing prior to his arrival. Steve Martin, like My mentor, like me, was probably there at that non-descript diner, eating some eggs and having an exhale from what was most likely a pretty jam-packed rest of his day. Maybe Steve Martin would've been thrilled to hear how he inspired much of my life philosophy, so much so that without *The Jerk*, I probably wouldn't have had the balls to be friends with someone like (gosh, I wished I could just tell you his name). Maybe he would have smiled politely and cut off the conversation with a glance at his watch and a wave for the check, telling me, "I'm late, all the best." Who knows and for that matter, who cares?

As I left the diner and walked downtown towards my office, I realized, it doesn't matter if Steve Martin knows I exist, nor does it matter if he missed an opportunity to meet his biggest fan. I needed Steve Martin/Navin Johnson to remain my hero forever. Any interaction would have most likely been underwhelming, given the almost forty-year buildup. What may read as defeat, I viewed as opportunity, because that day my hero remained in place, I'm going to boldly say, forever. In the end, the idea of Steve Martin as Navin Johnson is what makes me happy. And that's when I also realized that maybe what makes Steve Martin happy is not a crazy-eyed meeting with his biggest fan but just some peace and quiet over poached eggs.

Maybe we both got exactly what we wanted.

Thank You Notes
I Never Wrote

Occasionally, my mother will confess
something that she wishes she could've done
better, as it pertains to her parenting skills.

And while my sister and I disagree with
her on most of her imagined parental short-
comings, as she was truly one of the most
selfless, loving mothers there could be, there's
one missed life lesson we both have to admit
was never passed down to us.

"I should have taught you both how to
write thank you notes."

Bingo. In fact, I am horrible at writing
thank you notes. I first realized this when
I got to college and received one from my
new best friend Annie, my peer, someone my

own age who had their own stationery, even with their own monogram. Annie seemed to write me thank you notes minutes after we returned from an outing. "Thank you for the beautiful lunch at Taco Bell. Your generosity knows no limits." Or "Thank you for spotting me for that extra beer at The Pub, even though you took it from my hands shortly thereafter to pour over your own head before taking that stage dive; it was your original thought that counted."

I never wrote thank you notes for anything, including—*gulp*—after my own wedding.

I tried so hard to find lovely ways to thank people for pots, sheets, and coffee makers but it just seemed disingenuous, not because I wasn't grateful, but really, did we need additional paperwork to prove it? I preferred to invite them over for a meal cooked in the beautiful Le Creuset they gifted me or pour them a cup of coffee from the delightful Breville coffee machine that made such a delicious frothy foam. Would it have been weird if I invited them to come sleep with me on their gifted bed sheets?

Ok, maybe I should've written thank you notes.

When did my ineptitude in this form of etiquette hit me the hardest? The most soul-crushing day at the mailbox? My rock bottom, with letter opener in hand? It was when I received a thank you note for my daughter from one of her friends, a four-year-old, who already wrote a better thank you note (on her own stationary) than I was capable of cobbling together.

Dear Gala,

Thank you for doll and party.
Love, Sally

So here I am at the age of forty-seven trying to make amends, trying to get better about writing thoughtful notes and genuinely feeling sorry for all the notes I did not send to all the lovely and generous folks in my life that truly deserved them. Annie, if I sat down and wrote you notes for all you've done for me over the years, I'd wipe out an entire forest.

And how about those thank you notes for things that you didn't realize were gifts until way later in life? Notes to all the people (malicious or not) who end up teaching you life's biggest lessons?

Dear Stylist at Lemon Tree Hair Salon,

Thank you for giving me that horrible haircut that made me look exactly like Ralph

Macchio for a good portion of the 1980s. If it wasn't for you, I wouldn't have had to work so hard on making sure my adorable, zany personality shone through what was truly a hideous tonsorial don't.

Dear—nope! Not even giving you a fake name,

Thank you for inviting me over to your house to give you hand jobs, and always asking me to leave upon completion. Also, thanks for the crushing blow I received when you told me, "I really want to take you to the prom because you're funnier, smarter and more fun than—nope! not going to name her either—but she has a modeling contract in New York City so . . . duhhh." If not for you, I wouldn't have learned how not to care when I'm not the prettiest one in every room.

Dear guy in college who had three first names (and a numeral at the end of the last one),

Thank you for inviting me to your dorm room to listen to whale mating music while you tried to make out with me and convince me you were deep. I know I was naïve, but I can now spot a bullshit invite a mile away at this point and aquatic sex music is just . . . well, not my thing. Runner up thanks goes to the football player who tried get me to take a moonlit walk with him on a beach in the Bahamas after ten Jell-O shots on spring break in college, because drunk as a skunk or not, I realize I can still land a pretty withering kick in the balls when I need to.

Dear horrible talent rep,

Thank you for telling me that I didn't have a face for TV but that I was attractive enough for you to ask me to close the door so we could "talk more intimately." How naïve I was—I believed you could get anywhere with only hard work and talent.

Dear first boss at Nobu,

Thank you for telling me that I was the "most unreliable, inconsistent employee they ever had." You were, in fact, correct. Twenty-one-year old Mary had no idea what it meant to put in a proper day's work.

Dear horrible horrible lady boss at talent management agency,

Thank you for scaring me into realizing what I did not want to become. Thank you for throwing your prescription drugs bottles at me, letting me listen to you berate helpless spa workers for not waxing you correctly, and for doing the same to housekeepers who loaded a roll of toilet paper pointing in the wrong direction. It was your combination of entitlement, self-loathing and unhappiness that prompted me to need a palate cleanser for my soul and apply for that job as "Wish Granter" for the Make-A-Wish Foundation. Best job I ever had.

Dear Ryan,

Thank you for not being on social media. Just as importantly, thank you for teaching me that it's often the people who know you *the least* who have *the most* to say about you.

Dear Mary,

Hi, it's Mary. Thank you for finally starting to learn how to say no to things you really don't want to do. How much time have you wasted coming up with modern-day equivalents to "the dog ate my homework?" Doesn't it just feel better to speak the truth than walking with a fake limp or feigning laryngitis? Keep up the good work.

Ok, upon further reflection, one more.

Dear Mom,

Thank you for laughing and not cringing upon reading this essay and thinking I'm calling you out for not instructing your girls how to have manners. You gave us more than manners. You gave us a sense of goodness and showed us that cooking is love, always making time to listen is love and ending every one of our millions of daily phone calls by saying, "I love you, be careful" (a trait that I have picked up and used myself whenever I know a friend is flying or getting in the car to drive more than three miles). That's better than any monogram.

Love, Mary

The Six Degrees of Chris-Ta-Fa

I grew up very Italian. Italian-American, that is. We were the God-fearing, sauce on Sunday cooking, grandparents in the basement living, *al dente* spaghetti eating, white leather loving, *Goodfellas* on demand quoting, Alfa Romeo with the top-down driving, Sinatra on the radio listening, Italian-American kind. Need more visuals? The three wise men in our Christmas nativity were Sammy, Dino and Frank and while other kids my age were playing Barbies, I was playing with Noodles. Who's Noodles? He was my Han Solo action figure, whom I renamed after Robert DeNiro's character in *Once Upon a Time in America*. Yes, that kind of Italian-American.

I also grew up eighteen miles outside Manhattan, so when I returned from college and informed my parents that I would not be moving downstairs into the basement with my grandmother, but would in fact be living in the city that my father had, and I quote, "worked my whole life to get us out of," this was definitely an act of rebellion. I was promptly informed that if I left the once a week homemade chicken cutlet security of my childhood home for a life in the big city, I was on my own.

Did this scare me? Quite the opposite, it was invigorating. I was going to make my big dream come true. I was going to be an actress!

Life during my early years of city life was filled with auditions and with an equal amount of rejection. I lived on Gray's Papaya hot dogs (because they only cost a quarter) and did temp work at various restaurants and entertainment agencies, most notably: Nobu, HBO, Miramax, 3Arts Entertainment and William Morris. I placed myself on the periphery of all the bright spotlights which I desired so badly to shine upon my face. I yearned to receive the attention of a proper agent/manager or land a small part in an indie movie. Better yet, land a role on the new HBO series based on an Italian mob family from New Jersey, but don't let me get too far ahead of myself.

FIRST DEGREE: She's Here So Much She Could Be a Stool

While chasing all these dreams, I was living in the West Village with my then-boy-friend, soon-to-be husband Ryan. Our friend Barret turned us on to this amazing little bar in Chelsea called Ciel Rouge, or what we called The Red Ceiling (as opposed to its correct translation, Red Sky). We quickly made it our go-to watering hole. Behind the bar was a handsome bartender, who felt so familiar to me that I used to say to Ryan, "He looks like we could be related. I bet he's Sicilian." He was a man of few words, who poured drinks, smoked cigarettes, and DJ'd the best music from CDs he pulled from a large tower. Who was this bartender? A young, not yet discovered by the entire world, Michael Imperioli.

These were our professional drinking days, so if we ever spoke a word to Michael, outside of a quick pleasantry, it was with a slur at best. But I'm sure we ordered enough vodka sodas to keep the red sky lit up and his CD collection restocked.

After late nights there I'd wake up most mornings bleary-eyed, and barely made it on time to my now permanent gig as an assistant at one of the best talent agencies in town. At the time I worked there they represented some of the biggest stars of the day, including Keanu Reeves, Chris Rock, Mike Myers and the entire cast of *Saturday Night Live*. Other than answering the phone, my job was to make coffee, which I did very poorly, and photocopy the daily casting notices called breakdowns, collate, staple and place on each of the four bosses' desks. I also read them intensely.

One day:

Italian American, female, 16-22, to play daughter of mob boss in untitled HBO drama.

It was as if God himself placed that breakdown for my eyes only. A part of my job was to take direction from my bosses with these breakdowns and place various headshots of the agency-represented talent into envelopes and send those out to the casting directors for consideration. So, what do I do? Well, life comes down to moments, right?

I placed my terribly cheap, homemade headshot with zero acting credits into the HBO Italian American female envelope along with the photos of the other Julliard-trained, Emmy winning, already-famous people that the agency pitched for the job.

And then, finally, in came The Call, which of course I answered because I was the assistant. But not only did I answer and patch through the casting director for *The Sopranos*

Sheila Jaffe to my boss, I was also still listening on headset, as the assistant's job is to take notes during calls.

I was primed to hear her say the words, "We found our Meadow Soprano and her name is Mary." Then my boss would run out from his office, rip off my headset, smash it to the ground and congratulate me on being so clever, claiming he had always seen a certain star quality in me.

It didn't exactly go down this way.

Sheila had called to inform my boss that someone in his office had also submitted her own headshot in the Meadow bunch and while they had a quick laugh about it, my boss' face was bright red and he glared at me from his open office door. He may have even thrown a pen at me.

SECOND DEGREE: Look at Me, I'm Famous-ish

But guess who did get a part on *The Sopranos*? Yup, our favorite Chelsea bartender broke through that red ceiling and into the stars.

In the meantime, I had embraced my catering calling and adapted a very Zen philosophy to my work: "If You Can't Join 'Em, Serve 'Em." I threw myself into opening one of the most successful catering companies in New York City, with a client list that read like a guest list for one of the best Oscar parties. In a way, I was having my own version of fame, so much so that the most famous party thrower in the city at the time, Denise Rich asked me to be her in-house caterer. This was a huge rite of passage in the crab cake world in which I dwelled as Denise's parties were legendary. She once actually turned the roof of her Manhattan building into an ice skating rink. During the time she called me her caterer, I served Stevie Wonder, Patty Labelle, Clive Davis, Liza Minnelli and many other notables.

One night, I was alone in Denise's living room doing one last pre-party check and the elevator opened to a guest who had arrived a few minutes early. Who should walk out? Michael Imperioli, now known to the world as Chris-ta-fa! We stared at each other, exchanging a familiar smile. I'm sure he did not remember me as the girl who hung out at his bar so often I could have been called a stool, but for a minute, I thought he might have run through the "Who's that? She looks familiar to me." "I bet she's Sicilian." Yeah, maybe he did.

There were a lot of famous people there that night, and one of the greatest gifts my career gives me are these special glimpses. Stepping back at the party and observing people from all walks of life. And in this sea of boldface names, I was transfixed by Michael and his wife. They held themselves back from the madness, having a good time, but not caught up in it. I was reminded of how far he had come and yet, he kept his friendly, approachable style. Of course, this led me to a "would have, could have" moment, spiked with a "I should have worked harder. Did I give up too soon? Was I really as happy with this pivot in my dream or was I pretending to be happy?" I mean, people like Denise Rich were hiring me, shouldn't that have been enough?

From that night forward, I started to fantasize about how I could take this new gift of a career and infuse it a little bit more with what I wanted to do outside of serving crab cakes. Tackling different aspects of media through my catering company's strengths became my new goal. Accomplishments that could appease the performer in me. I wasn't so zen anymore about only serving and never joining. I set off on another path.

THIRD DEGREE: Opening Night Finger Food

After the Denise Rich party, Michael Imperioli and his wife started a theater in Chelsea named Studio Dante and asked me, via Denise's assistant, to cater the opening. I can't remember the name of the production, but strangely, I remember that there was corn involved, and more importantly, I remember being more excited about this gig than any other glittery event I had in the works. I was back in a theater started by true theater folks, my people or at least the people I so desperately wanted to let me into their club. That gig got me back into dreaming about theater and performance. Yes, he was one of the stars of the biggest hits television had ever seen but watching him in action and seeing him first hand and his obvious love of theater reminded me how a mad love like that pushes you to drop all logic and chase your dream. Settling would feel like some form of death.

A few days after that theater opening, I sat down to write my own play, *If You Can't Join 'Em Serve 'Em*. Think "David Sedaris serving food at his sold out readings." That was the vibe I was going for. I dreamt of a packed house where the audience would sit and listen to me read my hilarious and heartfelt stories, while my waiters passed them mini bite-sized nibbles of whatever food or drink reference on cue.

FOURTH DEGREE: These Were the Bad Times

And while *If You Can't Join 'Em Serve 'Em* still sits in a folder on my laptop, I did expand to other platforms. I published books and got myself on television as a "party expert," catching the eye of some of the biggest names in my industry such as Ina Garten and Rachael Ray. These food dynamos and their interest in me not only opened doors, but personally, it felt like they gave me "the nod." If they could believe in me, I could believe in myself.

One night, about ten years into being known as "Caterer to the Stars," I was seated next to Mario Batali at a charity dinner. At the precise moment the auctioneer announced a dinner for ten cooked by Mario was up for grabs with a starting bid of $50,000, he leaned over, introduced himself and asked me, "Are you the caterer I keep hearing about?"

Before he could reconsider that he must be mistaken, I stammered, "Yes I am!"

"You know, I could say yes to a lot more of these charity dinners if I had a caterer to do them with me." As the gavel hit the podium, we shook hands, and our catering collaboration began. We called it Mario by Mary.

Mario brought me into his fold, including me on trips with him and his chefs to various charity events and openings. And while this was the ultimate stop for many in the food world, this come up happened during one of the darkest times for me, in both my career and my personal life. While I loved glimpsing the world behind Mario's very electrifying purview when we first met, it was a dark time. For years I had been dealing with side effects from powerful doses of fertility drugs, and the subsequent disappointments I suffered from multiple pregnancy losses. I was in mental and physical pain due to crippling endometriosis that was causing my infertility. I was miserable, distracted, deeply unhappy and as a result, losing touch with the company I started with so much promise and passion. As a result, I started to overly enjoy what seemed like a never-ending cocktail hour to numb and distract myself. This went hand-in-hand with the good stuff, the validation I felt in being part of Mario's superstar posse. Yes, I was on my way professionally. Except that nothing about this voyage felt right personally.

Shortly after the much welcomed birth of my daughter, Mario asked me and a few trusted others to join him on a trip to the opening of his Eataly emporium in Los Angeles. I had also been in talks with some of the team at Eataly about creating a party *hors d'oeuvres* line for LA Awards season, so the trip was two-fold. Putting aside my personal and physical issues, I packed my bags for one last Mario trip, ready to ride the high of it all.

Mario was on top of the world back then. There on the opening day of Eataly, I watched him give a VIP tour for some of the biggest names on the planet, doing what came so naturally: waxing poetic about food and making everyone in his orbit feel like a welcomed pal at his proverbial table. As this tour continued, a publicist whom I knew from my early catering days pulled me aside to deliver a quiet but powerful blow. "Heads up," she warned me. "Things for Mario are going to get rough. Not sure his team is equipped to handle what's ahead."

While I had heard rumors of an impending takedown, her words cut me like a knife. I felt physically sick. Making my way to the front doors of Eataly to get some air, who do I see casually walking through the entrance amidst a sea of other high-profile celebrities?

Michael Imperioli.

It had been years since Denise Rich's apartment and his theater opening. Both of us were older, and I guess, wiser, but he seemed so peaceful. I noticed he was wearing Mala prayer beads. There was a noticeable Zen to his cadence, again walking a few steps away from all the madness, taking in one moment at a time, at his pace. He looked healthy, and, compared to where I was in my life, he definitely seemed happier?

Again, it made me stop and think. Was I on the right path? Was it time to get off this Ferris wheel of endless parties, and stop seeking attention from something that felt inauthentic and, from what the publicist had just warned me about, would be potentially downright scary? Who was I really, and who did I want to be?

FIFTH DEGREE: Accidental Neighbors

A few years later, I returned to the city after a Covid-inspired stint upstate that I thought might be permanent but proved to be a short-lived chapter. We had subleased our Chelsea apartment, so a kind family from my daughter's school offered us a temporary home close to Central Park. One morning, while walking through the park and falling more and more in love with what would become our new neighborhood—Bada-Bing!

Michael Imperioli, walking with a Buddhist monk.

The next day I walked past him again and realized I simply cannot ignore these sightings as coincidence anymore. So, I dug a little deeper, first by going on Instagram to see if he had an account. I discovered that not only did he have an account, but based on a picture he posted, we were possibly living directly across the street from each other. But my favorite find: he and his wife had become meditation teachers.

SIXTH DEGREE: Everything Ends Virtually

New York City is one of the largest metropolises in the world, with nine million people living and loving, day after day. Therefore, what are the chances of running into a celebrity you admire? Very slim. The chances of running into that same celebrity twice in your lifetime, definitely slimmer. But what about when you run into that special someone repeatedly in a city this size, in different neighborhoods and times of year, and even in other large cities at various pivotal times in your life?

This discovery more than piqued my curiosity; it prompted me to join Michael and his wife via Zoom, dabbling into my own Buddhist exploration. I eventually invited my husband to join me too, grateful that we have weathered much suffering together and are still open to growing with each other, grateful for the ups and downs of my career and his, finding compassion for those who wronged me, seeing all my experiences (even the toughest ones) as teachers while I attempt to walk a path towards enlightenment. Once again, the bartender from a Chelsea bar is my talisman, taking my order and expertly DJing the background music.

At one Zoom meeting Michael taught us a technique to stay present in meditation. He told us to imagine our practice as a clear sky, and when any stray thought enters, we should pretend it's a cloud and just blow it away with our minds. I love this imagery and work diligently at this practice, but just so you know I'm also not taking myself too seriously here, as a neophyte meditation student. Let me tell you what cloud keeps popping into my peaceful sky, week after week, during these meditations?

That I would have made an excellent Meadow Soprano.

Strangers
With Hot Dogs

The year my last book *Tiny Hot Dogs* came out, I decided it would be a good idea to show up to strangers' homes with hot dogs and vodka. This little creative experience was part of my book tour journey, an idea sprung from two of my favorite television moments: Ed McMahon knocking on the doors of strangers and handing them checks the size of Buicks via a direct marketing relic called "Publishers Clearing House Sweepstakes" and Oprah casually knocking on a doors of strangers and causing them to either cry or faint or both.

Don't get me wrong; while it's a well-known fact that I enjoy my endless delusions of grandeur, I don't think I'm in the same league as Ed or Oprah. However, I do love a good surprise and since my first book, *The Cocktail Party*, my entertaining and party-preparedness tome, didn't break any publishing records, this time, I was taking matters into my own hands.

So I announced on Instagram:

"Purchase twelve copies of *Tiny Hot Dogs* and I'll show up at your book club!" And, ever true to my love of 80s infomercials, I tossed in a "but wait, there's more" promise: Instead of ginsu knives, I'd show up with pigs in a blanket and shakers of martinis.

I never expected anyone beyond my mom and some of her friends to take me up on this offer—but what do you know? Strangers by the dozens wanted me to come to their homes.

"You're crazy!" said my business partner/ husband, watching me map the distance to places like Parsippany, New Jersey and Allentown, Pennsylvania.

"How far is Nova Scotia? Actually, where is Nova Scotia? Does that mean a plane?"

"You're not really going to just show up at strangers' homes with cocktails and *hors d'oeuvres*, are you?"

Eye rolls and mutterings of "she's nuts" followed me wherever I went, until the day I set off for my first visit.

I promised both my other business partner and my husband that I would check in with them once I arrived at my destination so they could confirm I would not be chopped up into a million tiny hot dogs. It all felt very hooker-like, with them as my pimps. We even created a safe word: raccoon (or just its emoji if I was really in trouble) which I could text them to call the police.

First stop? Somewhere in Massachusetts.

I stood before a beautiful suburban home in the middle of the state in a town I had visited once before with my parents and Grandmother Lucille. Grandma Lu accidentally lost her dentures on the side of the highway because the long drive from Montauk to Boston made her vomit from car sickness, so it was kind of hard to forget.

Ding dong.

I was nervous and a little sweaty, holding the vodka and large tray of pigs in a blanket, as well as slightly concerned that I smelled like pigs in a blanket (the smell of cooked hotdogs had permeated my car during the four hour drive). I certainly did not have the adrenaline rush I anticipated Ed and Oprah enjoyed while waiting to yell "Surprise!"

When the hostess arrived at the door, I was surprised at how incredibly warm and gracious she was, welcoming me into her beautiful home and into a kitchen that looked plucked out of a Goop inspiration board. I was greeted by ten happy faces and was beyond touched to look around and see that each of them had made a recipe from the book. I started to realize they were slightly nervous at the thought of meeting me?

"Is it just like your mother's?" A pretty blonde woman wearing a shirt that read "One martini, two martini, three martini floor."

"It's perfect. Nance would be proud," I responded quickly before even tasting a piece of my mom's friend Rita's chocolate cake, a recipe I had included in the book.

"Oh I loved that chapter about your Mother, especially the don't try cocaine advice."

"The closest Nance ever got to cocaine was the powdered sugar she put on this cake," I announced to a big laugh. I was loving this, totally in my element.

"Can I make anyone a martini?" I offered since this is what I had promised them.

One by one they shouted out their orders, dirty ones, dry ones, neat ones. I made a note to bring an actual bartender with me on the next trip.

Once the martinis were served and the little piggies devoured, the questions began:

"What did Robert DeNiro say to you?"

"Is Bradley Cooper tall in real life?"

"Who was on the private plane with you that almost crashed?"

"Who's the worst celebrity you ever worked for?"

On the second martini, we got deeper: infertility, marriage, work/life balance and dreams either in progress or unfulfilled.

I was impressed with how quickly we all dropped our guards and how quickly these women were to tell me their "secrets." This felt like sitting around with girlfriends I knew for years, not strangers. I don't think I was ever this honest with my "real" girlfriends. It was intoxicating even if I wasn't—I always swapped water for vodka for my second martini; this wasn't supposed to turn into a slumber party.

With this first event such an out-of-the-gate success, I felt bad telling them I only had one hour to stay (a safety net I put in place to get out of any weird situations). But I extended this first visit and almost all my visits after that beyond my self-imposed curfew because each stop proved unique and magical in different ways. I was greeted with amazing things: John Goodman cocktail stirrers, Alec Baldwin "schweddy ball" recipes, a screening of *The*

Jerk (my favorite movie and if you haven't seen it, you're really not living your best life). At one home I was greeted by a beautiful custom cake made in the likeness of my book cover. This was one of the largest gaggles, about thirty women, all ready not only to ask a lot of questions, but share their lives with me.

Dare I say it, I had a hit on my hands? And, dare I admit: I was getting addicted to this type of gathering, that spanned from, "Let's invite the girl from New York City who can tell us if Bethany Frankel is really an asshole," to tears and hugs and real-life advice with both old pals and new. Guards were let down—way down—and laughter rattled like ice in shakers.

On that first night as I left the idyllic town limits, I was going over all the many intimate conversations I had just been a part of when I was reminded of what Aruni had once told me. On the first day we arrived at the retreat center we were all just nameless faces in sweatpants, sitting in a circle on the floor and preparing to spill our darkest secrets.

"There will be no one better to give you advice than a stranger," Aruni told us.

So it began then, as it began again and again with these nitrite and vodka infused house calls. Strangers will in fact give you the best advice.

Even better than your mother, father, siblings or best friends. Strangers will tell you the truth, whether you like it or not. What exactly do they have to lose? Forrest Gump told his entire life story, his innermost secrets, anxieties, triumphs, and failures to a bench full of strangers. And of course there were chocolates.

But sadly, just two months into my new dopamine world tour, it was all instantly taken away from me once Covid hit. Suddenly we were forced to quarantine with the furthest thing from strangers—our families!

The sadness, anxiety, and depression caused by this loss of interaction was real. The lack of connection to the outside world overwhelmed me and the second we were released back into the wild, I ran through the streets of New York, proclaiming that I would *"Never ever* leave you *again!"* One day I shocked Ryan when I almost kissed my favorite Central Park hot dog vendor smack on the lips.

I'm looking forward to getting back out on the road with this book, with this newly found appreciation for you who are at this point strangers. I'm still happy to supply the hot dogs and vodka, but more than that, I promise I'll arrive with a much deeper appreciation for your kindness, your open homes and hearts.

But until that moment I ring your doorbell, promise to step outside your comfort zone and do the same. Strike up a conversation with your dry cleaner, take a new mom or dad at school out to coffee or show up to the bus stop with a box of chocolates and a few hours of free time. You never know what you're going to get.

And I'll promise that this time on my current tour, I won't hold anything back. I'll even answer that "who's the worst client you ever worked with" question that I would usually shrug off with my stock answer.

"I've been so lucky to have mostly wonderful interactions with all my clients."

It's a new world. I'm ready to tell you who really sucks.

Put Your Pants On, Fran

"Abandon the search for truth;
settle for a good fantasy."—Fran Lebowitz

Prologue: If You Can't Join 'Em ... Serve 'Em

My career as a sought-after New York City caterer affords me an incredible opportunity to meet almost all of my idols. This does not come as a surprise to me, because as a child, I believed I had some sort of magical power that allowed me to manifest encounters with just about anyone of my choosing. This started early on, when I would sit in front of the TV and screen kiss (on the lips) the current object of my affection—Fonzie from *Happy Days* or Jo from *The Facts of Life*. Whether as a child or an adult, there has always been very little difference between the "real world" and the world that exists in my (highly active) imagination.

Now instead of a television screen standing between myself and my idols, there is a silver tray of mini hot dogs.

Oh, the places that tray has taken me! Onto billionaire's yachts and private planes, into the most highly coveted film and television premieres, and exotic places like Gwyneth Paltrow's hedges, Bradley Cooper's coat closet and, yes, even Carolina Herrera's kitchen behind her kitchen (yup, that's a real thing).

And while I never made it onto the stage or screen, I realized that by coming up with the most creative and clever food and beverage experiences to celebrate a client's new film or product launch, I was actually telling food and beverage stories for my clients, And then executing them. So what am I? Yes, of course a caterer, but my imagination has pushed me into a much greater role. Because, at my core, I am a born storyteller, and let me tell you, I've told and created some of the greatest food and beverage stories NYC has ever seen and tasted.

PART 1: Pretend It's a City—Again!

And then, in early 2020, Covid stopped the world! I left my beloved New York City to try out a simple life in the country until, on what felt like Day 255, when I realized I had mastered the art of melting cheese onto cheese for my own amusement and expanding my usually small frame into my now size M/L underwear. I was jolted out of my stupor when Netflix aired Martin Scorsese's *Pretend It's A City* (sidebar: Marty and I are from the same town in Sicily, as I tearfully informed him one night at a party, stepping between him and the buffet).

And . . . there she was.

My Fran. Fran Lebowitz, a goddamn American treasure. The Fran who penned *Metropolitan Life,* a first edition sitting on my shelf in a place of honor, a talisman and reminder that I am a fucking New Yorker. Fran gets me and all the things I love about this city that have made me who I am. After bingeing on the Scorsese flick, I started to really examine and re-affirm my relationship with my beloved city, and I realized it was time to jump back in. It was time to return to New York. And this filmic love letter to a still (and always) cranky Fran was my jumpstart. And while I didn't get up and kiss the screen, I alerted my husband and daughter that it was time to get out of our pajamas and head home. On April 1, we moved back to Manhattan.

And what do you know? On April 6, I got the call that events were back, and Sotheby's wanted me to cater their "Back to New York" dinner for their top clients. The guest of honor? My Fran.

So, not only would I pull off a triumphant return to catering at the most prestigious art auction house in the world, but for New York's grumpiest dinner guest. A challenge I was totally up for. I was determined to tell one of the greatest food stories NY had ever seen. It was as if writing that menu was my most passionate love letter to NYC, and to Fran.

The anticipation I had built up going into that night was, dare I say, hysterical and not in the amusing kind of way. More like the frenetic and obsessive kind of way. I thought of nothing else for weeks, aside from how Fran was going to fall in love with me. Would it be from that one bite of our caviar on knish first course? (A daring choice but, yes it worked.) I had no doubt that My Fran and I were going to fall deeply in love.

So, Mary, how did it go?

Well, after setting a perfect room and making sure every single bite looked fantastic, I started pacing, anticipating Fran's arrival. When the text came into my phone that she was in the building, I nearly dropped my pigs in a blanket.

"Mary, can one of your waiters bring an iced coffee to Fran on the 7th floor?"

One of my waiters?

Um, hell no. That would be me delivering Fran her coffee, and no one else. I assembled the most beautiful tray of iced coffee New York had ever seen and awkwardly carried it up to the 7th floor (my waiters are such better servers than me).

When the elevator opened, I took a deep breath and arrived at the moment I had manifested on my couch just a few months prior.

"Fran, this is Mary Giuliani, the caterer for this evening."

I stood there proud, iced coffee and silver tray in hand, her loyal servant.

She looked up from signing her books, eyeing me with a look only a New Yorker understands, and said, "What did you just say?" Used to all sorts of comments about my (huge sigh) last name, I sheepishly offered, "It's Mary, not Mayor."

"Oh good, because I thought she said, Rudy Giuliani was catering the dinner tonight. You should lead with Mary."

She immediately went back to her books and poof! my moment with My Fran was over.

I placed the now sad, slightly sweating (were those tears?) iced coffee tray down and went back to the kitchen to begin the evening dinner service.

"What's wrong with you?" my business partner Michele asked as I entered the kitchen like Pinky crushed by the Fonz. No one knew my pain. Fran had broken my heart.

Dinner service went on and was beautifully received, and when the last dessert plate was cleared, I decided to reward myself with one of my cherished rituals, the single post-event cigarette (something I hadn't indulged in for almost two years). I took one last look at the room, allowed myself a tiny moment of victory, and made my way toward the elevators.

At the exact moment I pressed the down button, I saw that Fran was heading out too, escorted by the head of events for Sotheby's. We all got onto the elevator together, and I almost didn't hear her when she looked at me and said, "That was very good."

"You mean it, Fran? You're not just saying that?" I asked—ok, stammered.

"If I didn't like it, I would have just said 'thank you.'"

A burst of chutzpah came over me and I asked, "Are you allowed to have a smoke with the caterer?"

(Cut to . . . the Sotheby's event girl growing uneasy with my overstepping the customary vendor/star boundaries.)

"Honey, I'm a seventy-year-old woman who survived a pandemic, I can smoke with anyone I want."

And just like that—it was on!

When we got to the sidewalk, I realized the one cigarette I had in my pocket had broken. Fran graciously offered me one from her pack. I pretended not to be awestruck when I noticed she had one lucky (an upside-down cigarette) in her pack.

I had a lighter in my pocket, which was a long lighting wand we used to light hundreds of candles at events. I offered it up, hand shaking.

"Is that a blow torch? I'll use my lighter, thank you."

"Yes, that's smart. That would be a horrible headline. Giuliani—the caterer—blows up Fran Lebowitz outside Sotheby's."

She laughed. I made Fran Lebowitz laugh.

Smelling salts, please, and thank you.

What followed was some truly wonderful banter which could happen in this magical city, when someone in the entourage that gathered asked Fran a really good question: Is there a place in New York that you've always wanted to go but as of yet, haven't been? The whole group leaned in to hear her answer.

"Yes, there is a private dining club on MacDougal Street, across the street from my best friends, the Clementes, that I've always wanted to see."

What?

Though I'm not a member of any club (country, dining or otherwise), my grandfather and father were in fact members of this very same club.

Without skipping a beat, I said. "I'm a member," which was a small (major) fib as I personally was not yet a member but, ahem, the granddaughter/daughter of one.

"I'd love to take you as my guest." I chimed in again, like a schoolgirl asking the cutest boy in her grade to a coveted concert for which she has an extra ticket.

"I would like that. Can I bring the Clementes?"

"You can bring the Cohens, the Clementes, anyone you want."

Again, she laughed.

Then the awkward moment.

"So how do I get in touch with you to make this happen?" I asked. Noticing she has no phone, I start with, "Since you love my last name so much, this will be easy to remember, my email is ...@ marygiulaini.com."

"I don't have a computer."

Ahhh, right. Everyone knows this. I know this. Damnit.

Her car arrives and the Sotheby's events girl whisks her away and agrees to share my info with her "people." She hands me one last cigarette from her pack to enjoy after she leaves and off she goes.

So . . . now I wait.

PART 2: . . . and Wait

And let me tell you, I'm not very good at waiting because during this purgatory period I started really going overboard. I imagine all things me and Fran. I grow obsessed with the idea of what our new friendship will look like—it's definitely golden. The many restaurants and writing haunts we will visit. Trips to Snedens Landing along the Palisades in her 1979 Checker Marathon where she'll regale me with stories of her time with Toni Morrison. Casual dinner invites to "Marty's house" where she'll introduce me as "the other Sicilian from Polizzi."

I calmly inform my husband when he sees me eyeing up the cigarettes in the 7-11 that I'm going to have to become a smoker again (in the name of art, of course) because how could I possibly be the muse/best friend of Fran Lebowitz without a heavy smoking regimen? I even go as far as to start thinking about what my "hanging with Fran" look will be and decide, without question, that it includes a casually tossed-around-the-neck scarf and some sort of cool jacket and yes this friendship would become so meaningful to her that she would, finally, to the joy of all New York, finally finish her third book, thanking me in acknowledgments as "the kid who made me laugh."

And then . . .

PART 3: She Calls. Well, Not Exactly

It's her assistant who sounds very similar to her, so much so that I think for a moment, was this Fran pretending to be her own assistant? Which would be classic Fran, I immediately conclude, congratulating myself on my sleuthing. "Fran would like to take you up on your offer. Can her friends, the Clementes join too?"

"YES!" I triumphantly yelled, then hung up the phone and looked in the mirror. There was the girl who believes that mozzarella sticks are the greatest contribution to American cuisine. And now that girl would be rubbing elbows, trading quips and dining with New York City's literary and artistic elite. Holy shit, only in New York.

Oh wait! It hits me: I'm not actually a member of the private club where I just promised to host Fran and The Clementes.

What to do, what to do?

I begin the one-month process of becoming a member just so I can bring Fran as my guest. You are now reading the words written by the 22nd female member of the oldest Italian Heritage Club in New York City—thanks to my grandfather Charlie for paving the way. A day before this heaven-sent meet up date, which I had been referring to as "My Fran Period," the club called to confirm my reservation. They also reminded me of their very strict NO sneakers NO jeans dress code, firmly upheld since the club opened its doors in 1880.

No jeans. Fran only wears jeans.

I decide that my best approach is to appeal to the club's sense of responsibility to its members and who better to show some leniency than I, the 22nd woman. I beg: if they only just would relax the code for my guest this one time (not telling them who she is and just identifying her as "possibly the single most important guest I will ever walk through their doors," I promise to forevermore be the best toeing-the-line member in their midst.

Clearly, I'm persuasive, or they are amused by my begging, or just feel sorry for me. After some high-level calls are made to the club's board of directors, I am told they will make an exception, as long as the jeans are either black or "a very, very, very, dark denim." Terrified but hopeful, I share this news with Fran's assistant (or Fran, at this point I still suspect). She replies, somewhat firmly but in truth (it's probably why she's Fran's assistant in the first place), that pants or very, very, very dark denim will not be possible. Fran has only one type of jean and that's it.

Again, I beg.

Nope, Fran won't budge. I call the club and beg some more, but the club won't budge; they've already offered a compromise and now they don't give a shit who I may be bringing by. That's all. That's it.

I ask the assistant one last "Hail Mary" question, with fingers and toes crossed and rosary basically in hand, "Would Fran like to dine next door to the club at Villa Mosconi with me instead?" I am politely, but instantly, turned down, I concede defeat. Tears, a full tray of iced coffee glass tears, run down my face.

EPILOGUE: Still the Girl With the Tray of Tiny Hotdogs

Devastated was an understatement. I started reliving the moments on the sidewalk outside Sotheby's, when I made her laugh, and those tears kept streaming. It was real, wasn't it? She didn't just like me for my entrée to that fabled, old school club, right? She did want to know me for me, right? She did want to take those car rides to the Palisades, and call me her best friend? Right?

But no, I think it was just the club.

And while I could sit and wallow in what could've been/should've been, months and yes, a few therapy sessions later, I realized that the way this went down was exactly what gives this city the magical yin-yang of both wish-granter and soul crusher. New York is constantly put ting obstacles in your way to inspire, in fact, to demand that you work harder to get what you want. Sometimes you do.

Sometimes—lots of the time—you do not. I started to feel better, began thinking about all my career "almosts" as gifts instead of losses. I realized that, yes, like Fran and her jeans and like the club and its rules, I like where I am and am making no moves to shift to someone else's ideal. I'm a food and beverage storyteller, a granter of culinary wishes, who loves to start with anyone's "great idea" and make it come to life. I'm ok with that. In fact, I'm great with that. So what if I was always going to be the girl holding the tray of mini-hot dogs, hoping and wishing that one day one of these luminaries (Fran, Marty, the list goes on) will take it from my hands, set it off to the side and proclaim, "It's you, Mary" and not just ask me for directions to the coat check or if I can bring a Diet Coke to a VIP.

But Fran, if you're reading this: my offer still stands. Just think about putting on a pair of pants, will ya?

Acknowledgments

Thank you James Conrad at Golden Note-book Press for believing in me and this book. The moment I stepped into The Golden Notebook Bookstore, I knew you and Jackie Kellachan had created a uniquely special bookshop. Little did I know how special it would become for me. I'm honored to be your second published author but Golden Note-book Press will always be my number one!

Meg Thompson, *New York Magazine* is correct, you are the "sexiest book agent on the planet" but also the smartest and bravest and a true leader in publishing voices that matter. Because you believed in me all those years ago, I believed in me and what a journey it has been. Onto the next one . . . .

Abbe Aronson, third times a charm! You have turned every single dream living in my head into a reality. There is truly no better partner in business, creativity, words, laughter and friendship than you. Mrs. Weinberg would have loved that you kept this little dream alive. Here's to the next million great ideas we will bring to life.

Carol Ebbecke, thank you for your copy attention to every word, reference, punctuation and, well, burnt hot dog? Not an easy job!

Adrien Broom, thank you for always lending your creative, inspired mind and ginormous heart to your work. The photo shoot for this book was one of the best days of this journey. Thank you for seeing me for exactly who I am. And this cover? Magic.

Michele Pokowitz, Ryan Brown and my entire work family (both past and present) at MGCE for everything!!! When faced with losing this business, there was no one worth fighting for more than you. I am so proud of what we have all built and the little engine that could that continues to thrive. You are all so incredibly dynamic and talented in so many unique ways and I'm grateful you chose me to dream and create with.

To my precious friends that I NEVER EVER want to lose . . . . Annie Nugent, Lydia Fenet, Chudncy Ross, Stcfani Masry, Pearl Aday, Reyna Mastrosimone, Mindy Cohn, Anne Thornton, Rachael Ray, Grace Potter, David Burtka, Cindy Halliburton, Samantha Mathis, Mallory Page, Tara Fogarty-Graziano, Tommy Crudup, Kristen Shannon, Joanna Adler, Jane Scott Hodges, Adrienne Christos, Amy Beard, Kelly Powers, Lisa Vogel, Dana Cowin, Tripp Swanhaus, Jay Alaimo, Dylan Dreyer & Brian Fishcra, Lauren Balkin Cohen, Michelle Chin, Holly Parmelee, AJ Birchby, Ashley Burr, Elizabeth McCarthy and Lara Gad.

Aruni Futuronsky and all the kind strangers at Kripalu. Thank you Aruni for saving my life, not once, not twice, but three times. You are everything and more.

Scott Rosenberg, SOP, I adore you. Thank you for being my very special friend and for letting me write in your guest house, on your couch and in your backyard. Thank you for loving all three of us so deeply.

Dr. Masa Kanayama for healing with both your skilled surgical hands but also your heart. Thank you for being the first person to listen to my pain and validate it. I look forward to taking on this beast with you.

My Endosisters . . . your pain is real, your loss is tremendous and I will fight forever to make sure we are all healed and heard.

To the woman who gave me life the day she made me a mom. I will forever be grateful to you and your family for your strength, courage and generosity.

Michael Lang and Lee Blumer, even though you are gone, it is impossible for me not to thank you as you both turned on the light to all of my dreams. Save a spot for me up there.

Likewise...Grandma Mary, Grandma Lucille, Grandpa Charlie and Grandpa Franklin. I feel you with me every day of my life.

Uncle Richard, our family poet, thank you for seeing the artist in me at such a young age.

My incredible kiddos: Luke, Cole, Mia Johns and my Goddaughters Lucy Nugent and Eloise Delaney. That I get to be your special person forever is one of the greatest gifts in my life. You all blow my minds with your magnificence. Can't wait to hear the stories you write about me someday . . . be kind kids . . . be kind :)

The Giulianis (Charles, Pamela and Sister Sophie) I love you all so much and to the Giulianis who are not mad at me after reading the Mary NOT Mayor chapter. I am so proud to share a last name with such a wonderful bunch Grandma Evelyn, I miss you and am forever grateful of the time I got to spend in your kitchen.

The O'Briens (Tess aka Gigi) for your love always and to the O'Brien clan, what an incredible family, Queenie and Grandpa must smile everyday seeing the beauty they created with their love.

To the Jarmains and Nicchis for all the love, laughter and lasagna. Life without my aunts, uncles and cousins would be far less amazing. I adore all of you and each unique gift you have added to my life.

My sister Nanette, my light, my best friend, my heart. You are the wind beneath my wings, the mustard on my hot dog and the person who makes me believe that we can all truly change the world with compassion and kindness. Brother Eugene, there is no one I love laughing with more than YOU! Thank you for loving this crazy little family of ours.

Mom and Dad, I am the luckiest that I get to be called yours. Thank you for my beautiful life and teaching me the power of love, prayer and laughter.

Ryan and Gala . . . it's very simple . . . YOU ARE MY EVERYTHING!!!

Oh and Frankie Lebowitz Giuliani and the kind girl in Puerto Rico that found you. We did not rescue you, you rescued us. Thank you for peacefully lying at my feet while I wrote this book and for patiently waiting for me to take you out for a walk while I was caught up in a chapter.

Two-time author Mary Giuliani (*The Cocktail Party: Eat, Drink, Play, Recover* and *Tiny Hot Dogs: A Memoir in Small Bites*) is a lifestyle expert and Founder & CEO of Mary Giuliani Catering & Events (MGCE). Mary is a born food and beverage storyteller who has created parties for the *crème de la crème* of the art, fashion, and entertainment set for over twenty years, earning her the moniker "Caterer To The Stars."

In addition to founding MGCE, Mary has appeared on *Billions*, *The Barefoot Contessa*, *The Today Show*, *Good Morning America* and is a featured regular on *The Rachael Ray Show*; Mary's column "Eat, Drink & Be Mary" also appeared in *Rachael Ray In Season* magazine.

Mary graduated from Georgetown University with a degree in English/Theater and lives in New York City with her husband and daughter.

Cover design by Rodrigo Corral Studio
Cover photography by Adrien Broom